The Legend of Zelda: Majora's Mask

The Legend of Zelda: Majora's Mask

Gabe Durham

Boss Fight Books
Los Angeles, CA
bossfightbooks.com

ISBN 13: 978-1-940535-26-5
First Printing: 2020

Series Editor: Gabe Durham
Associate Editor: Michael P. Williams
Book Design by Cory Schmitz
Page Design by Christopher Moyer & Lori Colbeck

For Jenny and her boys

CONTENTS

A CURSED CARTRIDGE

I FIRST BECAME A FAN of *Majora's Mask* through a ghost story.

The game inspired a famous internet horror story—or creepypasta—called "Ben Drowned," told in the form of message board posts and videos made by a lone college student named Alex Hall and posted unceremoniously to a 4chan message board. On September 7, 2010, Hall made his first post—anonymous but for the username Jadusable—telling the story of how an old man at a garage sale gifted him a used Majora cartridge. Jadusable takes it home and finds the save file of a boy named Ben still on it. Even when he starts a new game, though, the characters continue calling him Ben. And when he deletes Ben's save file, the game doesn't take it well. The cartridge, we soon learn, is being haunted by the ghost of a dead boy.

What makes the story truly special are the videos Hall uploaded as proof of the haunting: In one, the protagonist Link begins to play a song on his ocarina and suddenly catches fire. In another, Link explores a cave with his entire torso contorted sideways as backwards music plays. In yet another, Link travels around Hyrule,

1

and no matter who he talks to—a treasure chest, an owl, a man in a mask shop—they all say the same spooky thing: *You shouldn't have done that…* Eventually, the ghost escapes the cartridge, infects Jadusable's computer, takes over his accounts, and endangers his life. The story ends on Jadusable's YouTube page, where his location on his profile has been changed to "Now I am everywhere."

"Ben Drowned" was fiction, but it didn't feel like it to readers. By the time I discovered the story, it had reached a level of popularity rarely seen in creepypasta. (As I research the story, Walmart keeps trying to sell me an adult-sized Ben Drowned mask for $17 in Google ads.)

Hall has since explained how he used a *Majora* ROM and a Nintendo 64 emulator to create convincing scenes in which the game goes terribly wrong. Hall told Kotaku in 2017 that he chose *Majora* as the haunted game for its apocalyptic themes and "creepy atmosphere." Indeed, the videos maintain a creepiness that feels native to the game itself, as if revealing a layer of intrigue that was in *Majora* all along. Even without watching the "Ben Drowned" videos, it's hard not to feel as if maybe every *Majora* cartridge is a little bit cursed.

Not that I knew it from experience. The game came out in my high school days, when new preoccupations began to compete with video games for my attention. I'd taken up violin. I was either dating or trying to be. I was at the height of participation in my church youth group while also beginning to write edgy short stories inspired by Chuck

Palahniuk. And, in the middle of my parents' ongoing divorce, I'd developed a talent for performing my own okayness to the world, which was an exhausting lie to keep up. When word of a new Zelda game got to me, I thought, "So soon after the last one?" and didn't give it a second look.

Majora is the sixth entry in Nintendo's popular Legend of Zelda series, released for the Nintendo 64 in 2000 in the long shadow of its immediate predecessor, 1998's *Ocarina of Time*—a bestseller many were already calling the greatest video game of all time.

Majora's Mask never boasted the sales numbers or critical coronation *Ocarina* did, but over the years *Majora* earned a fiercely devoted fanbase, culminating in a 2015 remaster for the 3DS that offered a new generation of Zelda fans a portal to *Majora's* land of Termina for the first time, as well as a chance for those who'd played *Majora* as kids a chance to turn back the clock and try the game anew. Yet I still hadn't played it.

My own entry point into "Ben Drowned" and then *Majora* itself finally came from a 2017 longform article Victor Luckerson published in the Ringer called "The Cult of 'Zelda: Majora's Mask'," which explores how *Majora's* reputation went from "the N64 Zelda game that isn't *Ocarina of Time*" to cult favorite. "*Majora's Mask* is a strange game that has launched even stranger subcultures," Luckerson wrote, "and found itself resurfacing, again and again, in unusual and sometimes horrific contexts."

Soon, I was downloading *Majora* onto my Wii U and then tracking down a 3DS to play it on the go. The game and its community finally had my attention.

•

The story of *Majora's Mask* begins after the events of *Ocarina*. Link travels deep into a forest in search of his fairy friend, Navi, only to have his horse and ocarina stolen from him by the mischievous masked Skull Kid. Link chases the thief down a deep hole and into another dimension—the land of Termina—where Skull Kid turns Link into a Deku Scrub, a kind of cute little tree goblin. We soon learn that Skull Kid is being controlled through the mask he's wearing by the evil spirit Majora, who has set Termina's moon on a collision course that will destroy the planet in three days.[1] But just before the world ends, Link retrieves his time-bending ocarina and uses it to turn back the clock 72 hours, where the shadowy Happy Mask Salesman turns Link back into a human. It is up to Link to fight his way through the four main regions of Termina to awaken each of the four godlike giants who can stop the moon in its tracks.

---

1   Unless the player is really on her game, Link will likely spend the first three-day cycle exploring and chatting with townsfolk. In this case, you'll run out the clock and watch the fiery apocalypse for yourself before being transported back to the beginning of the first day.

Link must turn back the clock and reset the three-day cycle again and again, as many times as it takes, until all four giants have been summoned and Majora is defeated.

However, a simple plot description does not accurately convey the wild missions you find yourself completing in the game. You defend a ranch's cows from being abducted by ghost-aliens, play guitar in a band of Zora fishpeople, lead baby chicks in a march that rapidly ages them into adults, and help the thong-clad spirit of a dance instructor "bring the world together and stir it into a giant melting pot" by passing on his dance moves.

And while *Majora* boasts a big, explorable world, missions often take place in the relatively small central hub of Clock Town. There, you meet many of Termina's inhabitants, all of whom are aware that the moon in the sky grows larger by the minute. Depending on when you talk to these characters within the three-day cycle, you catch them at different moments of dealing with the looming apocalypse—and the different decisions each character makes in how they want to spend their last days. The honesty with which these heart-wrenching interactions are depicted was rare for video games of the 00s, and remains rare for Nintendo, a company who typically likes its games light and cheerful.

This book is about both how *Majora* was made and how *Majora* has been received by its fans, and it's about what happens when we examine these two things simultaneously.

Majora's Mask is perfect for this sort of study because (1) it's one of the most-interpreted video games in existence, and (2) we know a lot about how it was made. The developers were interviewed when the original game came out in 2000, again when it was remade for 3DS in 2015, and many times in between. It doesn't hurt that *Majora*'s producer (Shigeru Miyamoto) and two directors (Eiji Aonuma and Yoshiaki Koizumi) are, by most counts, the three most famous developers in this history of Nintendo, or that the game was mostly scored by Koji Kondo, Nintendo's most famous composer.

Where do we find meaning in this much-beloved, much-analyzed game? In the creators' intentions? In the fans' interpretation? Or merely in the game itself?

To answer this question, we're going to look at how the game's directors' taste has impacted the Zelda series; how *Majora* builds and sustains mystery; how fans have interpreted the game and why those interpretations are so creative and varied; how *Majora* was made from the parts of its predecessor; what inspired the development team while they made it; how *Majora* was localized for and marketed to the West; how the game's legacy has changed since its release; and which of *Majora*'s themes, if any, we all can agree on. Each of these topics will allow us to further investigate the relationship between how *Majora* was created and how it was received—and shine a light on the strange and tumultuous romance between art and fandom.

THE STORY GUYS

If I had to present an insultingly reductive dividing line for both gamers and game designers, it would go like this: There are story people and there are mechanics people.

Shigeru Miyamoto—creator of Link, Zelda, Ganon, and Hyrule—is a mechanics guy through and through. When the Zelda franchise began, Miyamoto wanted to make colorful, absorbing action games that pushed the limits of hardware and tradition. He didn't care about the good guy's inner turmoil or the evil pig-wizard's motives—he just wanted the game to be epic and creative and satisfying and fun.

To all the story lovers, Miyamoto offered a single "story screen" to accompany his first game in the series, *The Legend of Zelda*. In its famously garbled original English translation, that story reads:

> MANY YEARS AGO PRINCE DARKNESS
> " **GANNON** " STOLE ONE OF THE
> **TRIFORCE** WITH POWER. PRINCESS
> **ZELDA** HAD ONE OF THE TRIFORCE

WITH WISDOM. SHE DIVIDED IT
INTO " **8** "UNITS TO HIDE IT FROM
" **GANNON** " BEFORE SHE WAS
CAPTURED. GO FIND THE "**8** "UNITS
" **LINK** " TO SAVE HER.

If you clean up the translation, the original Japanese reads something like,

DON'T WORRY ABOUT THE " **STORY** "

Miyamoto has said as much in interviews about his philosophy. "When you're playing a game, the story is there to give the big world you're in some substance and meat," he told *Game Informer* in 2017. Story serves gameplay, not the other way around.

On the other end of the spectrum were Eiji Aonuma and Yoshiaki Koizumi. Today, they're two of the biggest names in the history of Nintendo. Aonuma is the longtime series producer of the Zelda games, responsible for overseeing monster hits like *The Wind Waker*, *Twilight Princess*, *Skyward Sword*, and *Breath of the Wild*. Koizumi, meanwhile, has overseen every major Mario outing from *Super Mario Sunshine* through *Super Mario Odyssey*. Koizumi was also one of two men (along with Shinya Takahashi) in charge of the development of the Nintendo Switch—Nintendo's fastest-selling console to date.

How did these two come to be entrusted with the keys to both of Nintendo's biggest franchises? The answer has a lot to do with the time they teamed up to create a Zelda game that had never been slated to exist; built it using a preexisting game engine, character models, and music; turned in the game on time and under budget; and delighted millions of fans—all while expanding the world's understanding of what a Nintendo game could be. But their beginnings at the company were much humbler.

•

Eiji Aonuma suspects that he got his job at Nintendo because he brought the elaborate mechanical dolls he'd made in college into his interview with Miyamoto. In his book *Power-Up*, games journalist Chris Kohler notes that Aonuma was "unknowingly replicating Miyamoto's own interview experience" with Nintendo's then-president Hiroshi Yamauchi, "in which [Miyamoto] brought his whimsical toys and creations to Yamauchi's office."

Aonuma's early days at Nintendo were spent drawing pixel characters in games like 1987's *Mario Open Golf* for the Famicom (eventually released in English years later as *NES Open Tournament Golf*). "When I started working at Nintendo, I actually didn't think I would be making games at all," he told 1UP in 2007. "I thought I was going to go into product design. So when I first started at Nintendo and Miyamoto asked me to do some character designs for games, it was a huge shock."

Part of that shock came from Aonuma's assumption that Miyamoto would prefer to work with people who actually played video games. For Miyamoto, though, hiring artists with backgrounds outside of gaming was not an accident. "I always look for designers who aren't super-passionate game fans," Miyamoto told the *New York Times* in 2017. To Miyamoto, the best way to deliver more innovative games was to hire people with "a lot of different interests and skill sets." And so he turned to Aonuma: an artist, chef, and bongo player with an easygoing temperament.

"I never played a game when I was young," Aonuma said in a conversation with *Dragon Quest IX* and *X* director Jin Fujisawa. "When I landed a job in Nintendo, I asked my girlfriend at that time, 'What is a video game?' And she lent me [the original] *Dragon Quest*." Aonuma fell in love with the game. "I stayed up all night to play it and she kept by my side the whole time coaching me, like, 'You need to go south five steps,' and, 'Now go to the east four steps.'"

From there, Aonuma discovered a love for text-based adventure games. "For someone like me who enjoyed reading stories," he said in a 2004 Game Developers Conference (GDC) talk, "these were games that allowed you to participate in the story and experience the joy of seeing your own thoughts and actions affect the progression of the story." Action games, however, were a much harder sell. "I was particularly bad at playing games that required quick reflexes."

The Legend of Zelda had recently come out on the Famicom when Aonuma began working at Nintendo, and he just couldn't get into it. "Immediately after I started playing the original *Zelda*, I failed to read the movements of the Octorok in the field and my game suddenly came to an end," he told the crowd at GDC. "Even after getting used to the controls, each time the screen rolled to a new area, a new Octorok appeared and I thought, 'Am I going to have to fight these things forever?'" Aonuma's takeaway: Zelda was not for him.

That is, until *The Legend of Zelda: A Link to the Past* (*ALttP*) arrived on the Super Famicom. As he played, he found himself enjoying cutting grass with his sword, opening doors with keys, and searching for treasures beneath stones—activities that had nothing to do with stabbing Octoroks. "I discovered that I was proceeding through the game," he said, "and I got the same feeling I did when using command inputs to actively participate in the story of a text-based adventure. I realized that those same feelings, coupled with a sense of play control response, far exceeded what I could experience through command input alone."

Aonuma has called *ALttP* his favorite Zelda game. It was the game that turned him onto the series in the first place—and one of the last Zelda games he was able to enjoy as merely a fan and not a creator.

It was fitting, then, that the first game Aonuma ever directed was the 1996 Super Famicom game *Marvelous: Another Treasure Island*, which looks and feels much like *ALttP*. *Marvelous* is a game where you control a team of three boys as they explore, swim, fish, and solve puzzles in search of pirate treasure, but with none of the traditional Zelda combat. While *Marvelous* was too late in the SNES life cycle to release in the West, the game was well-liked in Japan.

Perhaps most importantly, the game got Miyamoto's attention—and its similarity to *ALttP* was not lost on Miyamoto. According to Aonuma in a 2013 Spike TV interview, Miyamoto told Aonuma, "If you really want to make a Zelda game that bad, why don't you just actually make a Zelda game?" Apparently, this was both a sick burn and a legit offer. Aonuma came to work with Miyamoto on "Zelda 64," the Nintendo 64 game that eventually would become Link's first 3D adventure, *Ocarina of Time*.

And once Zelda grabbed ahold of Aonuma, it didn't let him go. Aonuma has never since directed or produced a non-Zelda game.

•

Yoshiaki Koizumi studied film in college but went to work at Nintendo immediately after. He, too, was a story guy. "My ambition had always been to make drama," he told Chris Kohler in a 2007 Wired interview. "That was my goal: Having a character, in a certain kind of world, having him go through a series of actions to accomplish something, and creating dramatic tension. Games seemed like a really good opportunity to create a kind of drama that you don't find in films."

Like Aonuma, Koizumi had struggled when playing action games. "I didn't get really far at all in *Super Mario Bros.*," he said. "I realized on World 1-1 that I wasn't really good at it at all. I kept dying. And it was at that point that it occurred to me, what do first-time players think of games like this? You jump right in and you just die over and over again."

And, like Aonuma, Koizumi did not begin his career as a video game superfan. When asked in a 2017 Reddit AMA for advice on how to break into the video game industry, Koizumi replied, "I think one of the best things that you can do would be to expose yourself to other kinds of play, not just video games. It will give you a well-rounded sense of the ideas that go around the concept of play." Koizumi, for instance, is very serious about pour-over coffee.

Koizumi's first gig was doing art, writing, and layout on the manual for *ALttP*. It turned out this job gave him more power over the game's lore than he'd known going into it. "What was funny was that at the time, it didn't seem like they'd really figured out what most of the game elements meant," he told Wired. "So it was up to me to come up with story and things while I was working on the manual."

Koizumi relished the opportunity. *ALttP*'s manual goes above and beyond the story padding of most manuals and opens with *a creation myth about the genesis of Hyrule itself.* "To set the stage for this adventure of the legendary Hero of Hyrule," the English-language manual begins, "it will be informative to delve into the Triforce myth, an ancient epic about the creation of the world that is still believed in the land of Hyrule." Apparently, establishing this ancient Hyrulean lore was a must for Koizumi because nothing gets gamers amped like the phrase "it will be informative to delve."

And delve it does. Well before any instructions about gameplay or enemies, the *ALttP* manual treats us to five pages of small-print backstory that starts with the beginning of time; moves on to the creation of the Triforce (the series's shiny MacGuffin that we are told holds "the essence of the gods"); and eventually focuses on the tale of Ganon's gang of thieves happening upon the Triforce "quite by accident," the ensuing "Imprisoning War" against Ganon, and the mystery of new disasters that have been temporarily halted by a

Ganon-y robed figure named Agahnim. The narrator's tone is breathless, as if recapping several seasons of a TV show that doesn't exist, but it's a recap that still makes time for some fun isolated moments—such as when Ganon steals the Triforce and his roaring laughter echoes across all of time and space. I'm sure *some* of this myth-making was ordered of Koizumi, but I'd bet that he took most of it upon himself in service of the worldbuilding and dramatic tension he'd always loved.

The bosses at Nintendo were happy enough with his work: They brought Koizumi back in to do the same for *Link's Awakening* on the Game Boy, released in 1993. This time, though, there was even more heavy lifting to do. When Koizumi came to work on *Link's Awakening*, he found that, even though the development team was deep into production, the game had neither a story nor much of a context. It was just Link going around a nameless island, stabbing enemies, solving puzzles, beating dungeons, and racking up heart containers. "So I ended up making an entire story to go along with the game," Koizumi said.

His initiative on *ALttP* and *Link's Awakening* is how Koizumi accidentally began his new career as a game developer. As he eventually put it in his Reddit AMA: "One day I had a manual that didn't have instructions for what should be in it, so I went to check with the development team, and next thing I knew I was working on a Zelda game."

15

Link's Awakening finds a shipwrecked Link washed ashore on Koholint Island—his first time leaving Hyrule in a Zelda game. To return home, Link must collect eight musical instruments to wake the mysterious Wind Fish—but, as he does, he learns of a rumor that the island only exists as a dream of the Wind Fish. It's a sweetly simple story, so its surreal twist makes for a nice wrinkle. Perhaps this is why *Link's Awakening* and *Majora's Mask* are fan favorites that are often mentioned in the same breath as one another—they're the playful yet melancholic oddballs that take place far away from all the canonical Hyrulean lore.[2]

"The dream, the island, that was all mine," Koizumi said. "And so that was my first experience doing the kind of work that we would now call 'event design.' But there were not too many people at the time with expertise in that area, so I really had free rein to do what I wanted, so long as I didn't make Miyamoto angry."

In fact, while working on *Link's Awakening*, Koizumi often felt as if he was the only one on the team who cared about story at all. "They were always saying, 'Let's not try to push the story forward too much.' So I would sort of

---

2 *Awakening* and *Majora* also stretch the full title's claim that each entry in the series is a "Legend of Zelda," a princess who appears nowhere in either game save for a quick flashback.

try to find sneaky ways to get it in without them noticing too much."

It's hard to imagine Koizumi having to sneak story into a Zelda game in the age where even 2017's *Breath of the Wild*, much praised for its narrative restraint, features a main quest in which you go around collecting pieces of your own backstory. But in the early days of Zelda, Hyrule had little history to speak of—and could have gone in many different directions.

Considering their history, it's wild that of everyone at Nintendo, it's Aonuma and Koizumi would go on to co-direct *Majora's Mask*, the first Zelda game for which Miyamoto was mostly hands-off. Why would the creator of a beloved action-adventure series hire such unrepentant story guys to muddy up the franchise with character, drama, history, and feelings? Miyamoto might have predicted that they'd create a Zelda game in which, for the first time ever, the action was far from the coolest thing about it.

DOWN THE RABBIT HOLE

MY EARLIEST ZELDA MEMORY, which still creeps me out, goes like this: When I was six, my parents rented *The Legend of Zelda* for me to play over the weekend. I went to bed thinking about it, and when I woke up the next day, I got out of bed, went straight to the TV in the living room, and played the game until my mom came in and found me. "Gabe, what are you doing up?" she said. "It's after midnight." I looked out the window: Sure enough, it was pitch black out. Somehow, I hadn't noticed.

For me, this memory takes on the unnerving quality of a nightmare. *Had I really missed the mark by eight hours? How could I not have noticed the darkness outside every window?*

•

Mystery is a slippery word. We tend to picture fog, trench coats, bassy synthesizers, untranslated symbols. Like Thriller, Comedy, and Horror, the genre of capital-M Mystery is classified by the effect it intends to have on its audience and is typically judged on how much of that effect it delivers. And yet the answer to the question "Why does this work feel mysterious?" can itself be a mystery.

Mystery is often created in narrative art by creating a problem and then not solving it—or at least not solving it yet. That's why mystery and crime pair so nicely: There's a dead guy on the kitchen floor. Who bludgeoned him? And with what? And why? The questions create a vacuum of possibility for audiences to fill with possible solutions from their own minds.

Chris Bachelder, one of my early writing mentors, used to say to students in his fiction workshop when we introduced a mysterious element in a story or novel, "You've just bought yourself some pages." What he meant was: Readers won't quit on you if they need answers. In music recording, the reason the fadeout gained such popularity for a time was that it created the illusion of the song drifting away from you, never allowing your brain the closure it thinks it wants—and so you must start the song over again.

It's fitting, then, that *Majora* begins in the Lost Woods, Hyrule's most traditionally mysterious location. In the original *Zelda*, it's the place on the map where you cycle endlessly until you traverse the woods in the correct sequence. In *ALttP*, it's full of thieves and dead-ends and fake Master Swords. It's the one area in *Breath of the Wild* that you can't paraglide into. In old folk stories, the woods are where wolves swallow grandmas and witches bake children into pies. In Arthur Miller's

The Crucible and the trials that inspired it, they're where the Devil was said to lure Puritans to their ruin. And in the 2015 film *The Witch*, the woods are where the Devil actually *does* lure the poor Puritans to their ruin.

But it's once Link has tumbled through those woods and into Termina that *Majora*'s true mysteries begin. After you fall, deeper and deeper, *Alice in Wonderland*-style, into a new dimension and your fall is broken by a large flower, you find yourself face to face with Skull Kid, who floats in the air with his fairies beside him, waiting for you. He rattles his mask at Link, who basically has a bad acid trip about being chased by a horde of what we know from *Ocarina* are called Deku scrubs—rhythmically swaying their leafy heads as they prepare to attack. Link takes off running, and then is chased by one enormous Deku many times Link's size, until it overwhelms him and us, its likeness taking up the whole screen. When Link wakes from his strange vision, he is a Deku scrub himself. He catches his reflection in the water and shakes his head in disbelief. Skull Kid tells Link he'll remain like this forever.

The nightmarish scene expertly uses cuts to make us feel Link's horror: We see the swarm of scrubs. We see Link's reaction. Then we see that the scrubs have somehow been replaced with one large scrub. It doesn't make literal sense, and so our brains go into overdrive picturing what Link himself must have seen.

A similar trick is employed minutes later by the scene in which Link meets the Happy Mask Salesman. The salesman is presented as a deeply ambiguous ally, one who wears a sick smile that seems to hide a darker motive. "You've met with a terrible fate, haven't you?" he asks, wringing his hands, and offers to help return you to your former self if you can get his mask back from Skull Kid. You're obligated to accept the help of this odd man who smiles when he's furious, and who may even share the blame for Termina's doom. Majora's Mask was stolen from him, after all—he should never have traveled with such dark magic, and probably should have destroyed the mask in the first place.

As the salesman monologues, the game highlights his unknowability by cutting quickly between shots of his mood swings, instead of transitioning between them, in what is described as a "non-linear dreamlike montage" by animator Jane Kernan. "It creates a sense that there's a story larger than those immediate parts," she explains, "and that those parts are all connected." The game trains us early on to understand that more is happening than what we are seeing and to envision what we might be missing.

Clock Town, meanwhile, is bursting with problems without obvious solutions. Each character has their own story (and often a quest for you to complete), but almost nobody spits out what you must do to further their story without you first putting in some detective work. The mailman seems so stressed out—how do I help him? The little person in the fox mask comes out when I ring the bell—how do I get him to talk to me? These dancing sisters seem dissatisfied with their routine—what can I possibly offer?

Majora offers the opposite of the directive-based quests of most adventure games, in which you know what you must do as soon as a distraught townie has finished lecturing: "Hello, young traveler! Won't you help an old lady? I seem to have misplaced my eight STRENGTH BOOST PIES. They are scattered throughout the city. I have added them to your MINIMAP."

Instead, you encounter people distracted by problems they would never expect you to fix. The citizens of Clock Town have no idea you're the famous Hero of Time in their sister dimension. You're just another kid. When the Clock Town guards offer you any respect at all, it's only because you have a big boy sword.

If you're playing *Majora* for the first time, it's impossible to tell which of these quests is critical. Should I stop everything and keep attempting the mailman's challenge of hitting the stopwatch in *exactly* ten seconds until I get it right? (That's what I did. How could I know there was a mask that would make the whole challenge much easier?) A sidequest is only revealed to be optional for the game's completion after you've finished it and received your measly heart piece—but even then, the quest may factor into the plot in ways yet to be revealed. There is a flatness to the game, an unwillingness to prioritize your objectives for you. Am I saving the world right now or simply doing a favor for a new friend?

The game quickly introduces new mysteries through its inclusion of collectible masks. When the Happy Mask Salesman turns you from a Deku scrub back into a human, you receive a mask that you can use to transform back into a Deku at will. Eventually, you will find three other "transformation masks," each with unique powers, that turn you into a Goron, a Zora, and, in an optional final quest for those who have collected all other masks, a "Fierce Deity." On top of the four transformation masks, there are twenty regular masks Link can wear that come in handy in specific situations: A cow mask gets you into the adults-only Milk Bar. A bomb mask lets you blow up whatever is nearby while also harming yourself (unless, in a trick I missed in my playthrough, you're crouching with your shield raised). A frog mask lets you talk to frogs.

Just as a series of quick cuts between scenes makes us picture what happened between them, masks make us picture what's beneath. "Just the idea that something is pretending to be something else is deeply disturbing," Kernan says, calling masks "false faces." "It's the forcing your imagination/subconscious to tell you what's behind there that creates this sense of dread or wonder generated by you. It's a more intense experience because of the participation."

This sense of dread is compounded whenever Link puts on one of the transformation masks. He does not casually pop it on as he does a normal mask; instead, the transformation mask seems to overtake him, and he screams in anguish. This happens *every time* you put on a transformation mask, and even after hours of play I never get used to it.

Game Informer eventually asked Aonuma why the masks hurt Link so much. He replied, "We're talking about masks that were created to contain the memories of people who have died. Often there are things they really wanted to do before they left this world, so becoming them is actually really painful because it's like hosting a really powerful spirit that's coming into you." Learning the answer in this case makes the masks even creepier—and makes the narrator's haunting in "Ben Drowned" feel all the more fitting. Ben lives on in a cartridge just as the Goron hero Darmani lives on in a mask.

To state the obvious: Each of these elements—unsettling masks, quick scenic cuts, and complex yet inessential quests—was the product of a decision the game's designers made, and each of these decisions caused additional work. Someone had to animate Link's anguished transformation face. Someone had to record his scream. Someone had to script how Link's surroundings momentarily go dark to better spotlight his pain. All in the service of tone.

And in addition to these deliberate choices, there is something mysterious about *all* 3D games of the N64 era because technology demanded a low polygon count of every person, place, and object in the game. We'd been through this transition once before with 2D games. 8-bit games asked us to imagine starships, dragons, and superheroes far more vivid than the sprite art depicted on the screen. The "realistic" box art style of *Mega Man*, *Crystalis*, *Contra*, and countless others is not mere false advertising (though it is that, a little) but is intended to be imaginational fodder for the player: *Think of this lifelike action hero when controlling the little blocky goober.* 2D art grew more detailed in the 16-bit era, but then resolution took a huge hit when games made the jump to 3D, as in the original *Star Fox*.

On the PS1, games found the power to portray 3D characters in detail—but only when you're not actually playing. In *Final Fantasy VII*, there's blocky Cloud running around town, the more detailed Cloud of battle screens, and the much more detailed Cloud who graces the pre-rendered full motion video cutscenes.

Majora doesn't attempt the *FF7* approach (and on the cartridge-based N64, it couldn't even if its creators wanted it to), instead exhibiting a consistent level of detail throughout the game that is the same in both cutscenes and gameplay. You miss out on the chance to see a "perfect" Link but gain the opportunity to bring your imagination to the party.

It's not a conscious effort—your brain improves upon the image automatically, filling in the gaps just as (to borrow an example from Scott McCloud's *Understanding Comics*) your brain sees a human face in every three-prong electrical outlet. The time I did mushrooms while camping with friends, I was delighted to find this particular ability suddenly working overtime: My brain reconfigured every cloud into a sort of cartoon animal while I laughed dumbly along—there's a friendly pig! And over there, a polar bear!

While we are all born with these associative powers, it becomes harder to access them as we wade deeper into adulthood. I remember playing the original *Metroid* on the NES for hours as a kid and then, when I finally leafed through the instruction manual, finding myself disagreeing with the artists' renderings of the in-game monsters. I'd already filled in the blanks myself, and I preferred my version.

Today, creators are exploiting low polygon counts to intentional frightening effect. The 2018 indie game *Paratopic* chooses PS1-era graphics for atmosphere and horror, making great use of pixelated textures to an impressionistic effect. To create an old, worn-out door, a designer must figure out how to create the illusion of age using big blocky pixels and a limited color palette.

Whereas high-budget contemporary games reward getting up close to an object to admire just how detailed it is, low-polygon games reward stepping a few paces back from an object to take in what the game's creators were going for—and then zooming back in to see how they achieved it.

While there's an unknowability to all blocky 3D games and pixelated 2D games, the mystery of good art does not come merely from a lack of specificity. Some people might think that good mystery lies in intentional vagueness, as if robbing a scene of detail makes a player think, "Wow, it could be anything!" but I believe the opposite is true. It's the highly specific choices that tend to get under our skin—when we can see that details have been chosen intentionally but we just can't figure out why.

"When most mysteries are solved, I feel tremendously let down," director David Lynch said in a 1997 interview with *Rolling Stone*, perhaps thinking of the time CBS forced him to name Laura Palmer's killer on *Twin Peaks*. "I want things to feel solved up to a point, but there's got to be a certain percentage left over to keep the dream going. It's like at the end of *Chinatown*: The guy says, 'Forget it, Jake, it's Chinatown.' You understand it, but you don't understand it, and it keeps that mystery alive. That's the most beautiful thing."

And that's how *Majora* sustains its mystery across dozens of hours of gameplay. It's full of details without over-explanations, and sometimes without explanations at all. A hand in a toilet asks for paper. How'd he get there? A nice scientist has somehow been turned into a Gibdo mummy. What experiment went so wrong? A mapmaker named Tingle floats on a balloon, dresses like Link, and has dreams of becoming a forest fairy. What's his entire deal? We never learn why aliens prey upon the poor Romani family. Or why the moon in this world has a face. Or where the evil spirit Majora came from (although Akira Himekawa's *Majora's Mask* manga offers an imaginative guess). Or what the Happy Mask Salesman's long game is. He leaves the game as beguiling as he entered it.

As a self-described Mechanics Person, I often spend adventure games skimming through text and skipping cutscenes to get back to the good stuff. But in *Majora*, everybody stops speaking before my curiosity has been satisfied. The game keeps buying itself some pages.

Even when you finally *are* victorious, the game ends without full resolution. Link returns to the Lost Woods, alone but for his horse, no closer to finding his friend Navi than he was when he began. The song ends not with a bang but with a fade-out. And the only way to try to scratch the itch, and—maybe this time—finally solve the mystery once and for all, is to reset the needle and start the song all over again.

BUILDING A 3D ZELDA

To TELL THE STORY OF *Majora's Mask*'s creation is to tell the story of *Ocarina of Time*'s creation—it's just that none of *Ocarina*'s developers knew in 1997 that they were creating the mechanics, assets, character models, and music for two games instead of one.

When it came time for work to begin on "Zelda 64," Yoshiaki Koizumi was only the third person Miyamoto added to the team, after Toru Osawa and Jin Ikeda. The pair didn't have much in place by the time Koizumi joined them except for the decision that Link's first 3D adventure would have "chanbara-style" fighting—the kind of sword fighting that appeared in samurai movies.

After his work on *Link's Awakening*, Koizumi had spent the rest of the SNES era creating graphics for the adorable *Super Mario World 2: Yoshi's Island*, and had most recently been promoted to the role of assistant director on *Super Mario 64*. He, along with Miyamoto, had been making notes for "Zelda 64" all throughout the fast-paced development of *Mario 64*.

Because the *Mario 64* team was not able to make the game nearly as large as they'd originally hoped, Koizumi said he was eager "to pour all those leftover ideas into *Ocarina of Time*." This included the unused idea of letting Mario ride a horse, which is how Link's steed was first conceived. And Koizumi already had a name: Epona, the goddess protector of horses, ponies, mules, and donkeys in Celtic/Gallo-Roman mythology.

"Zelda 64" was originally planned for the Nintendo 64DD, a peripheral disk drive add-on for the N64. The problem was that Link's moveset was so complex—containing about 500 patterns, according to Koizumi—that the magnetic disk struggled to find the right motion to correspond to the player's input, causing tremendous lag. So *Ocarina* would be released as a cartridge, an important decision for the game's legacy. The 64DD was a failure in Japan, and its release in the rest of the world was cancelled. If the team had released the game for the 64DD, we may not have gotten to play it.

Miyamoto went into the project unsure of how much game they could fit into an N64 cartridge, so they started by building the engine from a modified *Mario 64* engine. In Nintendo's popular "Iwata Asks" interview series, Miyamoto told Nintendo CEO Satoru Iwata that he was prepared for a worst-case scenario in which the entire game takes place inside Hyrule

Castle—just as all the levels in *Mario 64* technically take place inside Princess Peach's Castle.

Early on, Miyamoto suggested making *Ocarina* a first-person game. "But—while it wasn't very nice of me toward Miyamoto-san—I didn't try a first-person scene even once!" admitted Kozumi. "I was making the [character] model for Link, so I couldn't stand to see my Link not appear."

Link's character model originally had a silly button nose until Koizumi's wife remarked to her husband that all Nintendo characters had funny noses. "Don't you have any handsome ones?" she asked. So Koizumi narrowed Link's nose, pierced his ears, and cut back his sideburns.

At first, there was only "adult Link"—the comparably older version of Link that was still only said to be sixteen. "If you think about the chanbara [sword-fighting] element, that only made sense," Osawa said. "With a child form, the sword would be small and his reach too short, so he would be at a terrible disadvantage, especially against large enemies."

But Miyamoto and other staff members thought young Link would be cuter. "Link is a boy," Miyamoto said. "In the first game, *The Legend of Zelda*, he was about twelve years old. In *Zelda II: The Adventure of Link*, he was about sixteen, but I never wanted to make him just another cool hero. Until *Ocarina of Time*, Link was a playful and childish character." If you're like me, you're learning this for the first time. NES-era Link looks like he could be any age at all, though the North American booklet for the first game does call him a "young lad."

A new character model for young Link was created, but they still had adult Link sitting around. *Hmm,* they thought. *It'd be a shame not to use him.* Especially after Koizumi had gone to the trouble of handsome-ing Link up at his wife's request.

So the team landed on the one plot device that would allow them to have two Link character models in the same game: time travel. "We thought about how we could have both the child and adult forms appear in the same game," Osawa said, "and came up with the device of going seven years into the future by drawing the Master Sword and then returning back to his child form when he returns it to the pedestal." Time travel became the hook of the entire game—and one that nicely mirrored the Light World/Dark World mechanic of *A Link to the Past*.

The mechanic that made *Ocarina* so beloved and set up the time travel of *Majora* was originally created simply as an opportunity to use two good character models instead of having to pick one. Our most cherished stories sometimes arrive out of solutions to problems we, the audience, never knew existed.

•

Ocarina's camera began as a total mess. This was the early days of 3D, and the Mario and Zelda teams—determined to avoid relying on fixed camera angles—were tasked with solving problems nobody at Nintendo had ever had to solve before. For instance, how would the game handle situations in which multiple enemies were near Link at the same time? Would it be a free-for-all with all enemies attacking at once, even though some of those enemies might well be out of frame?

In the midst of dealing with these problems, the three-man team sought inspiration in a visit to Toei Kyoto Studio Park, which combines film studio tours with amusement park elements—kind of the Japanese equivalent of Universal Studios. It was a scorching summer day, so they ducked into an air-conditioned playhouse and caught a ninja show to cool off. "What caught my attention in the studio park was the sword fight," Koizumi told Iwata. He watched scene after scene in which twenty bad guys would surround the hero, and yet the hero would defeat them each time. Koizumi watched closely until he figured out the show's trick. "The enemies don't all attack at once," he said. "First, one attacks while the others wait. When the first guy goes down, the next one steps in, and so on."

This was the genesis of *Ocarina* and *Majora*'s influential Z-targeting system: When an enemy is nearby, you can press Z on the N64 controller to make Link directly face the enemy while the camera positions itself behind Link's back. Suddenly, it's a one-on-one fight, and all the other enemies back off until it's their turn. Locking onto enemies in this way has been endlessly refined since, but Z-targeting was a huge step forward in making 3D action games fun and fair to play.

•

As development continued, the *Ocarina* team slowly found its way—intimidated, yet excited by the sense of possibility in making a game on new hardware. Takumi Kawagoe, who worked on the in-game camera and cutscenes, likened the experience to "plunging into a pathless, misty expanse and thinking, 'I'm sure we can do this!'"

It was only then, with the early development stages finished and the team beginning to build the game itself, that Miyamoto taunted Eiji Aonuma into joining the *Ocarina* team as one of several directors. In a break from Nintendo's usual development style, work among the *Ocarina* team was divided up so that, as Aonuma put it, "multiple directors [were] responsible for individual portions of the game."

Aonuma's role was lead dungeon designer, which meant designing the layout of the dungeons as well as the enemies inside. The irony wasn't lost on Aonuma: The guy who'd quit the original *Zelda* because he was "so terrible at fighting creatures" was now the guy designing enemies. But what could he do? Enemies were important. "There was really no way for me to escape it," he said.

What he could do was create dungeons that were as much about strategy as they were about action. Aonuma was given free rein to build *Ocarina's* dungeons as he saw fit, and so he packed the dungeons with the elements of strategy and adventure that fascinated him most—giving each dungeon a theme, for instance, "such as rescuing trapped Goron[s] or hunting down the Poe sisters." Aonuma constructed the dungeons with a heavy emphasis on puzzles. "I love surprising people and I also like puzzles," Aonuma explained. "So I thought, 'It would be fun if the dungeons were full of puzzles." This element was a hit with fans, and set a huge precedent for Zelda games, including *Majora's Mask*, a game in which the dungeons are even more puzzle-dense than those in *Ocarina*.

Sometimes Koizumi and Aonuma's "story guy" visions clashed with Miyamoto's "mechanics guy" sensibility—particularly when it came to cutscenes. "This may be overstating it, but Miyamoto-san probably doesn't need any cutscenes at all," Koizumi said. And if the game *had* to have cutscenes, Miyamoto insisted they be rendered in-engine (instead of pre-rendered ahead of time) so that, as Koizumi put it, "he wants a way to redo them over and over."

Iwata agreed. "The last excuse he wants to listen to is, 'I can't fix it, because the cutscenes have already been made.'"

Meanwhile, anticipation for the first 3D Zelda continued to grow. The original plan was to release *Ocarina* one year after *Super Mario 64* and in time for Christmas 1997. In fact, it didn't come out until almost a year later, and Zelda fans grew irritable while waiting. In another of his "Iwata Asks" interviews, Satoru Iwata told the story of Miyamoto visiting the city of Kanazawa. "While he was there, he stopped by a convenience store," Iwata said. "Then the store clerk noticed Miyamoto-san and actually got mad at him, saying, 'Miyamoto-san! What are you doing here at a time like this!'" Miyamoto had no business traveling like normal person: He had a game to finish.

Every day, *Ocarina* went through massive changes. Part of the fun was that the team suspected, but didn't *know*, that it would all come together. "It was a mess right up to the end," Aonuma said affectionately. Koizumi agreed. "We didn't know what kind of game it was," he said, "until all the parts came together." For his part, Miyamoto places *Ocarina* alongside *Mario 64* as the two games he's had the most fun creating.

The game they came up with was a well-balanced blend of exploration, action, puzzles, and plot, with a simple hero's journey story and a horse that felt great to ride across the countryside. For better or worse, *Ocarina* was the perfect fan service for kids and adults who'd spent years closing their eyes and imagining how cool a 3D Zelda was going to be. When all the work was finally done, the team was able to take a step back and see they'd made something special.

But they were not prepared for when *Ocarina* came out and everybody lost their minds. 5/5 from *GamePro*. 10/10 from *Electronic Gaming Monthly*. A perfect 40/40 from Famitsu—the first N64 game to receive the rare honor. 10/10 from GameSpot—the site's first perfect score since its founding in 1996. A 9.5/10 from *Nintendo Power*. 10/10 from IGN, which raved, "If you're making games and you haven't played this game, then you're like a director who has never seen *Citizen Kane* or a musician who has never heard of Mozart."

It won Game of the Year awards/honors from the Academy of Interactive Arts & Sciences, BAFTA, Edge, EGM (in both the "critics" and "readers" categories), *Game Informer*, *GamePro*, GameSpot, and the Japan Game Awards. At 7.6 million copies sold, it became the 4th best-selling N64 game—only bested by *Super Mario 64*, *Mario Kart 64*, and *Goldeneye 007*. *Ocarina of Time* was a blockbuster hit, a critical darling, and a fan favorite.

So if you're Aonuma, Koizumi, and Miyamoto, riding high on one of the biggest successes of your career, and it's time to move on to the next game, how do you top *Ocarina*? More action? A bigger Hyrule? *Link gets a jetpack?* Or do you accept that there is no topping *Ocarina* and pivot hard into the Lost Woods in search of new magic?

PLAYING DETECTIVE

MAJORA'S MASK'S COMBINATION OF MELANCHOLY, mystery, playfulness, and heart have made the game one of the most talked about video games in the history of Arguing on the Internet—and never more than in the form of the fan theory.

The term "fan theory" can refer to a lot of different things. It can be as simple as your take on a character's motives in a movie or your attempt to iron out a particularly tricky plotline in a book—it is an interpretation, in other words, just as people have been interpreting art for thousands of years.

Usually, though, the term "fan theory" refers to a newer and more specific phenomenon, which the writer D.F. Lovett has usefully defined as "a form of contemporary critical theory, in which the audience analyzes the text and creates a new interpretation that explains 'what really happened,' creating a separate narrative aside from or within the narrative." Fan theories seek to follow a breadcrumb trail within the text itself to the

41

secret labyrinth beneath: *Zion is actually just another Matrix*, *the ending of* Taxi Driver *is actually Travis Bickle's dying fantasy*, *Ferris Bueller exists only in Cameron's imagination*, and so on.

There are numerous *Majora* fan theories to be found on message boards, fan sites, Reddit, YouTube, and elsewhere. A sample of these fan theories is as follows.

- *Majora* employs the most classic twist of all: It was just a dream.

- Skull Kid and Link are *the same person*: Skull Kid is a version of Link who has gone mad in the Lost Woods.

- Link and Tingle (the balloon-riding wannabe fairy) are *the same person* in different timelines, which explains why Tingle dresses so similarly to Link.

- The game's final temple, Stone Tower, is a symbol of the Tower of Babel story in the Bible.

- *Majora* takes place not after *Ocarina* but in the middle of it, in the time when Link is "locked away" for seven years, and this whole quest is how he trains to face Ganon.

- All of Termina was created by the spirit Majora so that Majora could detach from Skull Kid and instead possess Link's body—a more powerful host for Majora's dark powers.

- The events of *Majora* are actually a stage play, as in *Super Mario Bros. 3*.

- A black hole connects Termina to the worlds of both Star Fox and F-Zero.

- *Majora*'s Termina and *A Link Between Worlds*'s Lorule are both the Dark World from *A Link to the Past*. There have only ever been two dimensions—it's just the names that change.

- The four regions in Termina were built to perfectly correspond to the four Greek types of love: *philia*, *eros*, *agape*, and *storge*.

- The people of Ikana from *Majora* are actually the Dark Interlopers from *Twilight Princess*, a Zelda game that came out six years after *Majora*.

- Majora's Mask contains the spirit of Ghirahim, a villain who doesn't show up to the series until *Skyward Sword*, a Zelda game that came out eleven years after *Majora*.

- The Happy Mask Salesman is the Hero of Termina the way Link is the Hero of Hyrule.

- The Happy Mask Salesman, not Majora, is the game's true villain.

- The Fierce Deity (your badass final incarnation if you collect every mask in the game), not Majora, is the game's true villain.

- Even after Link defeats Majora, he and the citizens of Termina are cursed to continue reliving the same three days over and over.

The fan theory knows no maximum or minimum word count. A few of the examples above are from comments no longer than my summary: log in, theorize, mic drop. Others are painstakingly detailed, offering pages upon pages of justification. Likewise, some theories are dead serious while others seem more like playful performances. And some are merely shrugged at by fellow Zelda fans while others are debated fiercely.

Yet there is one *Majora's Mask* fan theory that stands tall above the others and appears to have been around longer than any others—it's the patient zero of *Majora* fan theories. As with many fan theories, the identity of this one's original author is lost to time. It's been passed around for years in a game of internet telephone, growing and changing and sprouting new theories. This process is not unusual. Fan theories often involve a social component—someone gets the ball rolling with a breathless message board post, and then others workshop it, argue with it, and make their own contributions. Eventually, someone massages the theory into a polished, exhaustive YouTube video.

The plot of *Majora*, according to this particular theory, was built around the Five Stages of Grief.

Formally known as the Kübler-Ross model, the five stages were documented by psychiatrist Elisabeth Kübler-Ross and eventually outlined in her 1969 book, *On Death and Dying*. The model, based on her time working with terminal patients, proposes that when people are coming to terms with either their own terminal illness or the death of a loved one, they tend to go through a pattern of emotions.

First comes **denial**. You don't believe what you're hearing. You can't be dying. *There must be some mistake.* Then comes **anger**. You find a person or a whole universe to blame for your bad fortune. *I've been a good person all my life—I don't deserve this!* Then comes **bargaining**. You let God know what great works you will achieve if only you survive. Or you let your doctor know how much money you can come up with to fight your prognosis with fancy surgery. *Everything is negotiable, right?* Then comes **depression**. You acknowledge your coming death, and the reality of it is crushing. *Why do anything?* You send your family out of the hospital room. You refuse lunch. Finally, you achieve **acceptance**. You calm down, settle your affairs, and try to make your final days count. *If there's not much time left, I've got a lot to do.*

The Five Stages of Grief theory is most often applied to *Majora* as follows: In Clock Town, especially on Day 1 of the cycle, you encounter several people who are in (stage #1) denial about the coming apocalypse. The most extreme example is Mutoh, the carpenter, who tries to convince the mayor not to call off the Carnival of Time, which is scheduled for the day after the moon hits the planet. "You cowards!" he says. "Do you actually believe the moon will fall? The confused towns-folk simply caused a panic by believing this ridiculous, groundless theory. […] You want answers? The answer is that the carnival should not be canceled!" True to his word, Mutoh stands alone in the Clock Town courtyard on Day 3 even after everyone else has fled.

After getting his Ocarina back, Link leaves Clock Town for outer Termina in search of the four giants, first heading south to the region of Woodfall. There, the Deku Princess has been captured and the Deku King mistakenly blames an innocent monkey for the crime. There are certainly many characters throughout the game who express (#2) anger, and the one that our theorists tend to point to is the Deku King's anger over his kidnapped daughter.

When Link defeats the evil Odolwa, the princess's true captor, and returns her to her father, Link leaves woodsy Woodfall for snowy Snowhead to the north. There, Link encounters the ghost of Darmani, a Goron hero who recently died while trying to save his people from perpetual winter. Not yet resigned to his own passing, Darmani attempts to (#3) bargain with Link. "I beg you!" he says. "Bring me back to life with your magic!" Sadly, mortality is one thing Link can't control.

After defeating the murderous mechanical bull-goat, Goht, and saving Snowhead, Link visits the Great Bay, where the aquatic Zora tribe is being terrorized by Gerudo pirates. There he meets Lulu, whose seven (fertilized) eggs have been stolen by the pirates. She's so (#4) depressed about her stolen babies that she's rendered speechless, and spends her days gazing out at the sea until Link rescues her kiddos and returns them to her.

Finally, there is (#5) acceptance, which our theorists attach to Link himself. On his final journey to the Stone Tower in the region of Ikana, Link receives the Light Arrows—a symbol of his own general en*light*enment (pun intended but not mine), or his understanding that he will never find his lost friend, Navi, or his acceptance of the possibility that he may just fail this dangerous mission and wind up dead along with the rest of Termina.

Proponents of the theory believe that the whole point of *Majora* is to take Link, and thus the player, on this journey through each stage to acceptance. And it's got its defenders. Dorkly's Tristan Cooper says "there's too much evidence to dismiss" the Stages of Grief Theory, Zelda Dungeon calls the theory "tremendously profound," Cracked rates it #1 on its list of "6 Insane Video Game Fan Theories (That Make Total Sense)," and popular YouTube channel The Game Theorists finds it so obviously true that they use it as the canonical foundation of a whole nother fan theory.

•

The last *Majora's Mask* fan theory we'll discuss, not as old as "Grief" but even more hotly debated among fans, is as follows: Link is dead for nearly the whole game. Also known as a *Sixth Sense* twist, "[Protagonist] is dead" is up there with "It was all a dream" as one of the most popular fan theories to apply to any game or movie. But for the *Majora* fan community, the theory's roots run deep.

"Link is Dead" is another theory where I can't say for certain who came up with it, but I can identify with confidence what popularized it: a 2013 YouTube video that's been seen 14 million (and counting) times by the Game Theorists, a channel with 2 billion views and the tagline "The Smartest Show in Gaming."

The creator and face of the Game Theorists is Matthew Patrick, or "MatPat" as he's called on the channel, a fresh-faced enthusiastic guy whose Twitter account (5.3 million followers) is earnest and life-coachy. MatPat is popular enough that in 2016 he met Pope Francis and gave him a copy of *Undertale*. Here's how I know my pop culture awareness is slipping as I slide into my mid-30s: I'd never heard of the guy until I began researching for this book.

The Game Theorists, which bills itself as a channel for people who "love overanalyzing video games," is a very YouTubey YouTube channel. The excitable host. The quick cuts. The relentless gags. The chiptune theme song. The bright colors. The guest appearances from other YouTubers. The series of fast-moving sight gags. The algorithmic fidelity toward doing videos on things that are popular right now. The accusations of uncredited use of other people's ideas. The beefs with haters. The reaction videos and the reaction-to-reaction videos. It's sugary and optimized and "just one more video" addictive. And late-stage capitalism is such that MatPat almost certainly makes more money than even the most senior designers of the games he makes videos about.

The video in question, called "Game Theory: Is Link Dead in *Majora's Mask*?" isolates the moment in the game's opening minutes during which Link falls down the psychedelic rabbit hole into Termina. The video argues that Link falls for so long he'd have to die on impact. "Nintendo has always taken falling very seriously in 3D Zeldas," MatPat informs us earnestly.

But first, the video begins by summarizing the "Stages of Grief" theory. And instead of taking the time to defend it, MatPat takes the "Stages of Grief" theory as a given for how the stages "perfectly match up" with the beats of this game. In this new context, Link is not grieving the loss of Navi or the heaviness of watching his new friends get smooshed by the moon again and again, he is coming to terms with the reality that he has died. Termina, then, is his own personal purgatory—a morality play created specifically for him.

The video's arguments for Link being dead are as follows:

- The name Termina suggests terminal, as in terminal illness. "That's not even subtle, Nintendo," he says, calling the name "a pretty big red flag."

- What happens in Termina seems to stay in Termina. Wouldn't Hyrule be also be affected by this End of the World Scenario if it were really happening?

- Epona would have died from the fall just like Link—but somehow, when you see her in Romani Ranch, she's fine, legs unbroken, ready to go.

- Link being dead explains why Termina is populated with variations on "real" people he's already met before in *Ocarina of Time*. MatPat's cohost, PeanutButterGamer, likens it to *The Wizard of Oz*, in which Dorothy's family and neighbors all show up in her Oz reality. "And you were there... and you were there..."

- Each of the transformation masks corresponds with a character who has died. You eventually learn an ocarina song, the Elegy of Emptiness, that creates clones of the dead transformation mask characters, but Link is ALSO able to create a clone of himself. Why? Because he, too, is dead.

- The "Link is Dead" theory squares with the official series timeline as stated in the 2011 Zelda bible *Hyrule Historia*. PeanutButterGamer notes that *Twilight Princess* (released in 2006 for Wii) follows *Majora* on the official timeline, and points to a scene in *Twilight Princess* in which Link encounters a previous incarnation of the Hero of Time who has now turned into a Stalfos skeleton. From there he cites a scene in *Ocarina* that states that people lost in the Lost Woods are fated to turn into Stalfos, so it follows that Link died in the Lost Woods in *Majora*.

- The mask salesman says, "You've met with a terrible fate, haven't you?" when he meets you and then again every time the moon hits the planet and repeats the cycle. The Happy Mask Salesman is telling Link he has already died. Heavy.

You've likely already been refuting the theory in your head as several others have done in response videos: *The many times Link falls and is fine in Zelda games. Hyrule and Termina are different dimensions. It's dumb for an argument to hinge on a game that came out years later.* Which may be why the video ends by offering itself the wiggle room of reminding us, as MatPat always does, that this theory is "just a theory." If "Five Stages" is the little snowball at the top of the mountain, "Link is Dead" is what happens as the growing snowball careens downhill. *Majora* is now not just a game that deals with death nor a subtle metaphor for grief—it's a secret purgatorial nightmare.

Unfortunately for fans of the theory, there is a rebuttal to "Link is Dead" and all the other fan theories we've covered so far. That rebuttal is the story of how *Majora's Mask* was made, a story not about dead heroes or encoded messages but about the need for speed.

365 DAYS TO
SAVE TERMINA

MAJORA'S MASK WAS NEVER SUPPOSED to exist.

Shigeru Miyamoto had a modest plan to squeeze a little more juice out of *Ocarina of Time*. He did not want to develop a new Zelda game, but instead a "Second Quest" remixed version of *Ocarina* much like the Second Quest in the original *Zelda*. The overworld would be a mirror image of the original, enemies would do double damage, and, most significantly, the dungeons would be completely rearranged.[3] Most of the work for this Second Quest would naturally fall on the shoulders of *Ocarina*'s dungeon designer, Eiji Aonuma.

But Aonuma wasn't interested in remixing his own dungeons immediately after making them, and he said

---

3 A version of the Second Quest, called "Ura Zelda" in development, was eventually developed and released as *The Legend of Zelda: Ocarina of Time Master Quest* for the GameCube and, much later, the 3DS.

as much to Miyamoto. So, according to Aonuma's telling in an "Iwata Asks" interview, Miyamoto offered Aonuma a far greater challenge: He wouldn't have to work on the Second Quest if he and a new team used the existing *Ocarina* engine and assets to build an entirely new Zelda game for the N64 in one year.

"Well!" Iwata replied in the interview, possibly hearing this part of the story for the first time. "So you're saying *Majora's Mask* was the result of your team picking up the gauntlet he'd thrown down?"

"Yes," said Aonuma. "That was the deal."

However, in a different "Iwata Asks" interview, Aonuma tells it this way: Miyamoto asked Aonuma to work on the Second Quest and Aonuma "hesitantly obliged" at first, but then "couldn't really get into it." So instead of working on the Second Quest, Aonuma began designing all-new dungeons that went way beyond remixes of existing *Ocarina* dungeons. "And that was much more fun to me," said Aonuma. "So I built up the courage to ask Miyamoto-san whether I could make a new game, and he replied by saying it's okay if I can make it in a year."

Despite his big ideas for a new game built from the *Ocarina* engine, Aonuma didn't know that he was talking his way into the role of the game's director. According to Aonuma in his GDC talk, the job kind of naturally fell into his lap. If Miyamoto himself was not going to direct the game (and he didn't want to), it was important that the job go to someone who already knew *Ocarina* inside and out.

As soon as he got the job, Aonuma felt the weight of it. "We were faced with the very difficult question," Aonuma said in his GDC talk, "of just what kind of game could follow *Ocarina of Time* and its worldwide sales of seven million units."

•

Because he had a much smaller team on the new game, Aonuma understood that the game would need to be smaller in scope than *Ocarina*. But he also knew that fans would be disappointed with a less ambitious game. Aonuma needed what he called "some clever idea" to bridge the distance between fan expectations and the team's limited resources.

Overwhelmed, Aonuma reached out to one of his fellow *Ocarina* directors. Yoshiaki Koizumi was already in the early stages of developing an exciting new board game for Nintendo about cops trying to catch robbers in a limited amount of time, "one where," as Aonuma put it, "you would play in a compact game world over and over again." Aonuma pitched the new Zelda game to him anyway.

According to Aonuma, Koizumi replied that he'd work on the new Zelda game "only if you let me do whatever I want to do." Aonuma agreed.

Immediately, Koizumi had ideas for how his cops-and-robbers game might solve Aonuma's problem of how to make a satisfying game in just one year. "I wanted to make it so that you technically had to catch the criminal within a week, but, in reality, you could finish the game in an hour," Koizumi explained in an interview with Hobo Nikkan Itoi Shinbun (aka "Hobonichi"), the online newspaper of *EarthBound* creator Shigesato Itoi. "I figured I'd just throw what I already had into *Majora's Mask*."

Aonuma liked Koizumi's idea. "If you played in the same places and enjoyed the same events over and over," Aonuma said, "we thought you might be able to create an entertaining game by giving it depth rather than breadth."

According to Aonuma in an interview with *Famitsu* (and eventually translated by VG Facts user Kewl0210), Koizumi's game was influenced by Tom Tykwer's 1998 German mind-trip thriller *Run Lola Run*. In fact, Aonuma said that Koizumi's pitch was simply, "What if we made something like [*Lola*] into a game?"

In the movie, a woman named Lola races through the streets of Berlin (over a charming and very European techno score) to come up with 100,000 Deutschmarks in twenty minutes to save her boyfriend Manni's life.

When Lola is shot and killed in the process, she inexplicably gets another shot at it, starting the clock over with twenty minutes to save Manni and memory enough of her last attempt to try a new tactic. When her second attempt gets Manni killed, she gets a third and final shot at it. It's like an old-school platformer brought to life: three chances to save the helpless boyfriend from a Big Bad.

Here, again, different interviews tell slightly different versions. In the Hobonichi interview, Miyamoto remembers seeing a trailer for *Lola* while *Majora* was already deep in development and thinking, "Oh, this is crazy!" because the idea was so close to theirs. When he watched the movie and found it to be much different than *Majora*, he relaxed.

Whether or not the movie directly inspired the game, it's interesting that *Lola* influenced *Majora* when video games themselves have so clearly influenced more recent time loop movies like *Source Code* and *Edge of Tomorrow*, in which a character must perform the same mission over and over until he or she finally succeeds. Movies inspire games that inspire movies that inspire more games as the wheel of influence continues to turn.

Conveniently, *Ocarina* already had a basic time system: The overworld had an internal clock with a sun that rose and set, causing different enemies to spawn depending on whether it was day or night. So Koizumi and Aonuma developed the concept of a cycle in which the game loops through the same three days over and over again.

Miyamoto was supportive of their idea and liked how the "replaying" mechanic squared with his belief that *all* games should be replayable. "It's useless to make something that the audience just skims over in one viewing, like a movie. The full flavor of a creation gradually emerges with each viewing, as all the subtleties reveal themselves."

At first, the team planned for an entire week to loop, but discovered that keeping track of the days would be a chore for players. "In this game the townspeople do different things each day and many different things happen," Aonuma said in "Iwata Asks," "but when the timespan becomes a week, that's just too much to remember. You can't simply remember who's where doing what on which day. […] When you returned to the first day, it was like, 'Do I have to go through an entire week again?'"

For a little while, Koizumi was still trying to divide time between *Majora* and other work. "At the time I started working on *Majora's Mask*," Koizumi said in the Hobonichi interview, "I had already been busy designing another game. I'm incredibly ambitious, you see. But then, Miyamoto…"

"Recalled you [to the *Majora* project]," said Miyamoto.

"I heard the whispers," Koizumi said. "*Zelda... Zelda... Zelda... !* And my game was canned! I was in shock."

Koizumi and Miyamoto are laughing as they tell it, but I get the sense that the game's cancellation was less funny to Koizumi when it happened. A challenge of telling a story based on interviews with Japanese game developers is that Japanese game developers are almost unfailingly polite. If you want to find examples of a current Nintendo employee being despondent over a cancelled game, all you can do is try to read between the lines of his "jokes."

It was not even clear at first what Koizumi's role would be. "When my other game design got scrapped and I was stuck back with the development team," he said, "I asked Miyamoto what I was supposed to do." Miyamoto's reply: "Do whatever you can!" Koizumi thought to himself, *That's not helpful at all!*

"I tried to work on things all by myself, but I had no choice [but to keep asking Koizumi to come back for more help]," Aonuma said in the same interview. "I couldn't have done it alone."

"The designs just got bigger and bigger," said Miyamoto.

Whether Koizumi liked it or not, Zelda was Nintendo's second biggest property—and a new Zelda game took precedence over other projects. So, if Aonuma needed Koizumi, he got him. This could be one of the reasons Koizumi went on to take charge of Nintendo's *first* biggest property. When you're creating a Mario game, nobody is pulling you off your project to work on something more important.

•

It took Koizumi and Aonuma a while to discover that Miyamoto was going to make good on his decision not to involve himself in the day-to-day work on *Majora's Mask*. This was partly because Miyamoto's role at Nintendo was changing so that he oversaw many simultaneous projects instead of focusing on one at a time. The year of *Majora*'s release, Miyamoto's name also appeared as either a producer or supervisor on *Kirby 64: The Crystal Shards*, *Mario Tennis*, *Paper Mario*, *Mario Party 3*, and *Pokémon Stadium 2*, and already he was at work on Nintendo's next console: the GameCube.

Nobody was used to this new arrangement, especially after the close daily attention Miyamoto gave to *Ocarina*. According to Koizumi, the team would whisper among themselves, "Miyamoto hasn't said a thing. He will eventually, right?" After all, Miyamoto had a history of suddenly demanding major changes, even late in development.

In his GDC talk, Aonuma speaks of Miyamoto as one who "upends the tea table"—a phrase he says is taken from a manga famous for a scene in which a stern, old-school Japanese father smacks his son so hard that the food flies off the table. Here, it's the game that gets smacked and the code that flies everywhere. "Whenever a game nears completion with only the final polish remaining," Aonuma said, "with no fail Mr. Miyamoto upends our tea table and the direction that we all thought we were going in suddenly changes dramatically."

Aonuma welcomes the input. "The time I have spent working with [Miyamoto] is even longer than my relationship with my father, so I really should be able to read his mind by now," he said in an interview, sourced by Nintendo Everything as originally appearing in *GamesTM*. "I am still surprised by his opinions, and I am far away from reaching Mr. Miyamoto's level of perspective. When you get to my age, the number of people pointing out your faults becomes quite limited. So in this sense too, I would like him to forever give opinions on the products that we create."

Miyamoto didn't always nail the balance of encouragement and criticism. At times, Miyamoto was the sort of "father" who withheld praise to keep his team working to impress him. "He never says, 'This is good' in the field," Aonuma told Dragon Quest's Jin Fujisawa in their conversation. "When Mr. Iwata was here, he would tell me that Mr. Miyamoto loved the game. But then I would go, 'What? He never told me that!'" It was not Aonuma's preferred way to be managed. "When I get a compliment, it would be reassurance and a relief for me. So I think there are pros to getting a compliment on your work."

But on this game, Miyamoto instead approached Aonuma and his team with trust and ease. If Miyamoto's presence can still be felt playing *Majora*, perhaps it is because he had already trained his staff well on previous games. Having worked with Miyamoto on *Ocarina*, Aonuma and his team were now upending their own tea tables.

SOMETHING INTERESTING, SOMETHING NEW

RUN LOLA RUN HEAVILY RELIED on a ticking clock: If Lola can't come up with the money in twenty minutes, Manni is dead. Aonuma and Koizumi knew *Majora's Mask* needed its own stakes to bring urgency to the three-day structure.

Thanks to a daydream of Koizumi's, this urgency came from an impending apocalypse. "I would look up at the moon and think about what would happen if the moon started to fall towards Earth," Koizumi said in an interview with *Official Nintendo Magazine*. "From that idea we moved on to the world in *Majora's Mask*, which is threatened by being destroyed by the moon."

The threat of the apocalypse soon went from a clever device to a real fear. On August 31, 1998, North Korea launched a rocket called the Taepodong-1, which flew directly over the north tip of Japan and then crashed into the Pacific Ocean. The rocket was actually a failed attempt at sending a satellite into orbit.

In Japan, though, the rocket came as a terrifying surprise. A *New York Times* article on the launch quotes retired Japanese Self Defense Forces general Toshiyuki Shikata: "The real reason for the North Korean missile is its target, which is Japan." In the immediate aftermath, a failed satellite launch looked a lot like a failed missile attack—and Japanese citizens wondered if this rocket was the beginning of a terrifying new war.

In the aftermath of the incident, Aonuma, Koizumi, and several others attended a colleague's wedding in South Korea. There, Aonuma and Koizumi discussed how weird it felt to, as Aonuma put it in a *Nintendo Dream* interview, "come to a wedding in a situation when missiles may fall down today." Here they were, feeling joy and celebrating love in the shadow of a potential apocalypse. For my generation and the next, this weird feeling is familiar: "Climate anxiety," or "eco-anxiety," refers to our worry about the devastating effects of climate change both already upon us and still to come. And yet we must still seek out the joy, fulfillment, community, and love that makes life in any generation worth living.

This contrast between terror and joy struck Aonuma and Koizumi as a rewarding theme to explore in their new Zelda game. They began to imagine a world of characters dealing with the end times, each in their own way. A mayor decides whether or not to cancel a carnival. A sword master cowers in the back of his training center. A bar's owner keeps his business open so he can face the end with his favorite customers.

Eventually, one of the ways they chose to explore this theme in the game was with an actual wedding. As Aonuma put it in an interview with Kotaku's Stephen Totilo, "We said to each other, 'I can't recall seeing a wedding portrayed in a game like this before. It would be really interesting if you had three days leading up to the wedding but there was this horrible cataclysm happening alongside it.'"

And so the "Anju and Kafei" quest was born.

When we meet Anju, the owner of Clock Town's Stock Pot Inn, she's distraught. She's supposed to get married in three days at the Carnival of Time, and her fiancé, Anju, has disappeared. We soon learn that Kafei had a run-in with Skull Kid, who transformed Kafei's adult body into the body of a small child. To make matters worse, a thief has stolen his ceremonial wedding mask, and he needs your help retrieving it before he can get married.

When you complete the game and defeat Majora, Anju and Kafei get married in Termina Field before all their friends and family. If you didn't finish their quest, Kafei is still child-size. You see Anju from Kafei's perspective, looking way up at his bride as they exchange vows. If you complete the quest, he's grown to his adult size. Again, you see Anju from Kafei's perspective, but this time it's eye-to-eye.[4]

Your long and demanding quest involves using the mail to send letters back and forth between the couple, finding and defeating the wedding mask thief, and personally attending their private wedding. Messing up a single step in the sequence means you must start over, and if you want *all* the items from the quest, you've got to do it twice. And yet the wedding is one of the sweetest stories in the game, even though (or perhaps because) it's got nothing to do with saving the world.

•

In *Ocarina of Time*, Link's ocarina is used to travel back and forth between the present day and seven years in the future. In *Majora*, the ocarina is instead used to move incrementally forward or all the way backward to the beginning of the game's three-day period.

Now that there was a device to turn back the clock and replay the same days over and over, the team had to figure out which of your items, if any, you would get to keep when you reset the clock. Ultimately, it was decided that you would keep your masks and your upgrades, but

---

4 This was both a clever touch and a way for a time-strapped development team to avoid designing an adult Anju for just one quick scene.

you lose your expendable inventory: your bombs, your arrows, your Deku nuts, and even your rupees.

In Nintendo Online Magazine, Miyamoto framed this decision as the team's greatest challenge—and one about which there was a "very heated discussion." But he said that taking away your items when winding back the clock offers a twist on previous Zelda titles so that "different joy could be sought."

"After returning to the original point," he explains, "why not make the game so that the people enjoy themselves by trying to figure out how to attain items the easiest way. To find the item again, an easier way, players can find joy."

For my part, I've never found this to be true. *Majora* is not a resource-management– heavy looter shooter or survival horror game, and having to hunt for items you had in your inventory moments ago does not demand a player's skill or creativity—it just makes you ask, "Where are the nearest pots I can smash?" Fortunately, the game is at least generous with resources.

Another time travel question was: Will time stop when you're in a dungeon? Miyamoto felt strongly that the clock should continue ticking. If a player entered a dungeon one minute before the apocalypse, it would be a shame if the player "could not feel the tension of the remaining one minute."

While the nonstop ticking clock adds tension, for some players it also makes the game stressful. "I'm prone to anxiety as it is," explained Leah Haydu on the podcast *Cane and Rinse*, "and I always felt tense while I was playing [*Majora's Mask*], always acutely conscious that if I missed something at a particular time of day in the cycle or (heaven forbid) ran out of time completely, I might end up doing a lot of things over again."

Playtesters at the Mario Club complained that "dungeons are something you have to think about thoroughly," Aonuma told Hobonichi, but the developers refused to budge—instead adding an ocarina song to slow down time. The clock would continue to tick, but slower and more gently.

•

Even when I take issue with some of *Majora*'s design decisions, I can respect that they were made from a desire to make a game that was new and interesting—a goal that's brought up every time a Zelda game is begun. New Zelda games are created by asking: What kind of play does the current generation of hardware allow?

The possibilities of 3D led to *Ocarina*, the possibilities of the Wiimote and its MotionPlus controller expansion led to *Skyward Sword*, the possibilities of the DS touchscreen led to *Phantom Hourglass*, and, although its full integration was ultimately scrapped, the possibilities of the Wii U controller led to *Breath of the Wild*'s Sheikah Slate. Even the original *Legend of Zelda* was built around the Disk System peripheral (and later, the Memory Management Controller chip in cartridges), which meant that a single adventure in Hyrule did not need to be completed in one sitting, but could stretch across days, weeks, months, and years.

Majora did not allow for such a question. The N64 was the same piece of hardware it had been since 1996 (though eventually a 4MB RAM expansion pak would open up subtle new possibilities). So instead, much of the developers' early conversations about *Majora* came from asking the same kinds of questions that Miyamoto and Koizumi asked themselves in the wake of *Super Mario 64*'s release: What are things that were included in *Ocarina* but not fully explored? What ideas did we have for *Ocarina* that we didn't have time to implement?

One of those ideas was *Ocarina*'s use of masks. In Hyrule Castle Town, there is a shop run by our friend the Happy Mask Salesman, who in *Ocarina* is nowhere near as creepy as he would one day become. Link can buy and wear a series of masks that change the way people regard him, but the game mostly treats the masks as objects to be given away: Find the gravekeeper and give him the spooky mask.

"So in *Majora's Mask*," Aonuma said in an "Iwata Asks" interview, "we felt it would be fun if Link himself transforms whenever he puts on those masks. [...] We felt that would expand the gameplay." They imagined a game in which Link uses masks not just to impersonate a Goron and Zora like in *Ocarina*, but to really become them—and they created a storyline to go with each transformation. "We made the game so Link could transform into Deku Link to fly in the air, Goron Link to roll across land, and Zora Link so that he could swim underwater." In the transformation masks, the team made a truly new contribution to the Zelda series.

This goal was echoed by the game's head script writer, Mitsuhiro Takano, in Nintendo Online Magazine. When asked whether he begins a game with character, story, or another element, Takano replied that the earliest concern with *Majora* was, "What kind of features are going to make *Majora's Mask* interesting?" Then they created characters to fit those features. Then they wrote dialogue to fit those characters. And then, *only then*, did they worry about plot. "Story was the last stage," he said, "so everything could be put together."

Aonuma has also said that the team tended to think of mechanics and motivations more than plot itself. Even the sadness of *Majora*, which feels like an artistic choice that needs not justify itself, is reframed by Aonuma according to how it affects gameplay. "When we talk about the feeling of sadness in a game like *Majora's Mask*," Aonuma told Kotaku, "for us ultimately it's something that we think about in terms of how it motivates the player. In this particular case, that really strong feeling of sadness makes you want to save this world."

Sometimes I wish that in interviews Aonuma would take ownership of his own artistry. To say "I made it sad to break players' hearts" instead of "We hope that the emotions the player feels for the townspeople will motivate the player to save the world." Yes, technically, I'm sure that's true, just as Francis Ford Coppola might say, "I made Michael Corleone such a complex character so that moviegoers would be motivated to stay in their seats and finish the movie." But what a weird circuitous justification for making something great. Don't apologize for your ambition, dude! We like it!

On the other hand, Aonuma's ordering of priorities is also how you make a game that is, foremost, a game. The original idea for *Majora* was not to create a mystical Zelda for fans to puzzle over for decades, but rather to do what Zelda games always do: Start with interesting mechanics, and then build a plot to justify those mechanics.

That's what's so cool about making art—you begin by making a couple of big decisions, and then those decisions inform new decisions, and then *those* decisions inform new decisions. Before you know it, it's the decisions themselves that are driving the car and you're just riding shotgun, giving directions from your phone, and trying to make sure the project doesn't run off the road.

That's why it's also so tricky to talk about your work as a creator. People ask you questions as if everything you did was *pure intention*—a series of capital-D Decisions. But if you're doing your job right, the game eventually develops itself.

THE ART OF THE REMIX

AT ONLY 30 TO 50 PEOPLE, *Majora's* development team was tiny compared to *Ocarina's*—and was made to work even harder.

Many decisions, then, had to be made quickly. According to Aonuma in *Nintendo Dream* magazine, the name Majora (or "Mujura" in Japanese) came from art director Takaya Imamura, who mashed up his own last name with characters from the movie title *Jumanji*. It sounded cool, so it stuck. It was only later in the process, though, that *Majora's Mask* was floated as a potential title.

The name Termina was not overthought, either. "Termina is a terminal, right?" explains Aonuma, inadvertently shooting down one of the "Link is Dead" arguments. "As it means a place where people come and go, terminal became Termina." Furthermore, the Japanese word for terminal, *tāminaru*, lacks the deathly connotations of the English "terminal."

A major timesaver was the *Majora* team's decision to use assets from *Ocarina*. When *Game Informer* asked whether this was more of an artistic decision or a time-saving decision, Aonuma replied that it was "a little bit of both."

"I think a lot of it comes down to those character models having the ability to express something that they couldn't in the setting of *Ocarina* because we had this very different image for the world where *Majora's Mask* takes place," Aonuma continued. By ripping the assets out of Hyrule and putting them into Termina, Aonuma's team made them feel fresh again. "Even though these characters have a similar appearance to the version of them that appeared in *Ocarina*, they express something different in a different world."

The team also felt that reusing assets would offer continuity between the two games. "If you think of the development process in terms of makeup," Miyamoto said, "we'd already laid down the foundation. All we had to do was layer everything else on top."

•

Another element from *Ocarina* that was remixed to great effect was the game's soundtrack. As with many of *Majora*'s assets, the *Majora* score is largely rearranged from Koji Kondo's original *Ocarina* score with some new songs mixed in. However, the soundtrack is not always as close to *Ocarina* as it might seem at first.

In a GameSpot interview, Kondo described his *Majora* score as largely Chinese-inspired. "When I saw the very first mask you see in *Majora*," Kondo said, "it really brought to mind for me, for whatever reason, a type of Chinese opera. The kind where the performers wear masks and the music is all percussive [makes the sound of a cymbal being struck rhythmically], and there's a lot of cymbals and bells and what not."

A new composition that stood out to Kondo was the theme that plays during the argument at the mayor's office. On Day One, you enter the mayor's office to an argument already in progress between the head guard, Captain Viscen, and the head carpenter, Mutoh, about whether the residents of Clock Town should evacuate. Kondo said he wanted the scene's score to "feel like that argument so that you'd have music pouring in from the left speaker and then music coming in from the right speaker," adding, "That back-and-forth was a lot of fun to create."

Like the other members of the team, Kondo was largely left alone on *Majora* to compose and rearrange as he saw fit. "With *Majora*, the director didn't sit and say, 'This is the kind of music I want,'" says Kondo. "[Aonuma] wasn't super hands-on, so I was able to create the kind of music I thought was appropriate."

The only feedback Kondo remembers getting from Aonuma was in the scene in which you meet the Keaton fox, who asks you five quiz questions from the game—hard ones like "How many tiny cow figurines are there in Clock Town?" Aonuma told Kondo, "I'd actually like this to feel more Japanese," and so Kondo changed the score.

Despite the lack of direction, Kondo clearly understood that *Majora* was a darker Zelda game—as we can hear from the way that existing tunes were changed. *Majora*'s Termina Field theme, for instance, is a remix of *Ocarina*'s overworld theme, "Hyrule Field." It starts the same way as in *Ocarina* but complicates from there. 8-bit Music Theory's video essay "The Music of Zelda's Overworld" points out just how dissonant the new theme's accompaniment is, "featuring upbeat stabs and semitonal clusters that sound gross in a perfect way"—even as the melody and harmony remain unchanged. That is, until the end of the tune's A-section, when the whole song grinds to a halt, lingers on a II7 chord, transforms into a II7b9, then on to a iiidim, then finally a ivdim—in other words, going to a weird place and hanging out there awhile—before finally looping back around and restarting the melody. "A typical Zelda melody with surprisingly dark undertones, eh?" says the video's narrator. "Sounds pretty *Majora's Mask* to me."

In another video essay, "Why Majora's Mask's Songs Are So Great," composer Jake Butineau points out that many of the songs Link learns in *Ocarina of Time* have a melodic pattern, whereas the songs he learns in *Majora* use the relatively dissonant tritone. The tritone is sometimes called "the Devil's Interval" for the despondent unresolved feeling it leaves in the listener. Butineu's video goes on to note that the *Majora* soundtrack generally contains more minor chords. The big difference between the games: "*Ocarina of Time* songs tend to give off an epic, adventurous vibe. *Majora's Mask* songs are more intimate."

Perhaps that's why the *Majora* score works so well when arranged for solo piano, as in Laura Intravia & Brendon Shapiro's remarkable *Shall We Play? Majora's Mask Piano Album*. In contrast, the full orchestral arrangements I've heard of *Majora*'s tunes are bloated and bombastic, robbing the score of its intimacy.

Nothing communicates the shifting tone of *Majora* like the game's three different Clock Town themes that line up with the game's three days. One of the first themes you hear in the game, "Clock Town Day 1," presents the score at its most lighthearted. Set to a light bongo and clipped tambourine, Day 1's instrumentation reminds me of Kondo's chill level 1-1 theme for *Super Mario Bros. 3*. And yet it's almost aggressively cheerful, mirroring many of Clock Town's inhabitants who have already been informed they are about to die but are going about their routines as if everything is wonderful. On Day 2, the tempo increases and the theme becomes slightly manic as life in Clock Town begins to unravel, and the percussion exits entirely to make way for the ambient downpour of rain. Day 3 in Clock Town is downright disturbing. An upbeat, almost frenzied version of the Clock Town theme plays while competing with long, ominous minor bass notes that do not pair naturally with the chords of the tune. It's like hearing two separate songs playing from competing car stereos. That is, until the darkness wins out: The evening of Day 3, the Clock Town melody recedes entirely and is instead replaced by a low foreboding synthesizer.

In an "Iwata Asks" conversation, Kondo describes the difference between composing for Mario and for Zelda. In a Mario game, you are controlling Mario, but Mario is not you. In a Zelda game, Link is you, and the music should help blur the line between the character and the player. "What's most important to me when making music for [a] Legend of Zelda [game] is generating an ambience expressing the situation and scene," he tells Iwata, who then restates it to Kondo's satisfaction: "The value of the music for you, Kondo-san, is less about how the melody is appreciated by itself than how well the sounds serve their purpose in the context of the game."

Aonuma says something similar about designing Zelda games in his interview with 1UP: "When a player is playing a Zelda game, my desire is for the player to truly become Link—that's why we named him Link, so the player is linked to the game and to the experience."[5] This also explains why Link doesn't really speak, even as other characters jabber at him constantly. "[I]f we did give him a voice, that would go against the whole notion of Link being you, because Link's voice should really be your voice."

This is one reason the emotional moments in *Majora's Mask* succeed: From the music to the dialogue to the gameplay, the game's creators have worked to bridge the distance between me and my avatar.

•

As the team worked to repurpose *Ocarina* assets into the new game, each member felt the freedom to check in with one another less often than they had on the previous game.

"I was responsible for the fairy-tale sections," said Aonuma in the Hobonichi interview, "and Koizumi was responsible for creating realistic depictions of the lives of the townspeople." In other words, Koizumi restricted

---

5 This claim may be more emotionally true than literally true. In an interview with French site GameKult, Miyamoto said that the name Link came from early design plans for the original *Legend of Zelda* in which "the game was to be set in both the past and the future. And as the main character would travel between both and be the link between them, they called him Link."

most of his work to Clock Town while Aonuma worked on the rest of Termina and the four dungeons. "I tried to emulate the fantasy atmosphere we had in *Ocarina of Time…*"

"And I created realistic lives for the characters," Koizumi said.

"You could say that Koizumi slapped his worldview on the whole thing," Aonuma said, laughing.

"I put in everything I've seen in my 30-something years on this earth," Koizumi agreed. "Aonuma was in charge of the outdoors, and when he saw how serious my town was, he made his areas of the game more lighthearted."

The exchange is a fascinating window into how Aonuma and Koizumi arrived at a balance. Often, when we compliment a game's tone, it's because the game's developers were able to maintain a consistent tone throughout: the unrelenting fear of *Prey*, the Chandleresque hardboiled cynicism of *LA Noire*, the madcap technicolor zaniness of *Katamari Damacy*. But what the *Majora* team achieved was a tone at war with itself. If you're brought down by the sinking mortal despair of the inhabitants of Clock Town, get out and go on an adventure. If you're sick of fighting, go back to town and insert yourself in someone's drama.

The team trusted that, even when embarking on a "classic" Zelda quest, you would take Clock Town's despair along with you. And if you ever forget, a quick look up at the constipated moon—drawing ever-nearer as the hours pass—is all you need to remind you of the world's ticking clock. This combination of light and dark is, to me, much of what makes *Majora* an artistically successful game. Unrelenting despair would be a drag. Unrelenting adventure would be *Ocarina of Time*. And *Ocarina* already existed.

•

The team's independence was partly by design. "My development teams are made up of people who know how to relax," Miyamoto bragged in the Hobonichi interview. But even if they had wanted to check in more often, there was simply not enough time to second-guess decisions.

In his conversation with Iwata, Aonuma mentions that it was when the team settled on the use of Deku, Goron, and Zora masks that the rest of the game's pieces came together. When Iwata muses, "It must have felt great when everything came into place," Aonuma replies, "Well, we really didn't have time so things had to fall in place!" It wasn't "first idea, best idea" so much as "first idea is all we've got time for."

When North American localizer Jason Leung met with the *Majora* team, he learned that "the team rarely got to go home." As Leung wrote in a diary entry for Nintendo.com, the developers took grim comfort in referencing their long hours in the game. "During the development process, the programmers would often say, 'Let's not bring my wife into this,' which was their way of saying that they didn't want to be reminded of their home life. They already felt bad that they were spending so much time at the office to work on perfecting the game. As a little in-joke, Mr. Takano scripted that the mayor in the game says, 'Let's not bring my wife into this,' during his exhausting, overlong council meeting."

Today, "crunch" in the video game industry is more commonly recognized as exploitation, leaving developers burned out and often undercompensated from overly demanding workweeks. In 2000, weary developers had to smuggle their complaints into the game itself.

Leung pointed out that "the game is filled with little winks" about the developers' busyness. The carpenters in Clock Town, for instance, who are building a tower for the Carnival of Time, "constantly wonder if they'll ever finish the job on time, and their musings are actually thinly-veiled reflections revealing the programmers' anxiety to finish developing the game according to schedule."

The absence from home life was especially noticeable for Takano, who was engaged and then married all while working on the game. "[*Majora*] was about being so tied up in work and not being able to tend to the things that are actually important to you," Leung told me in an interview. "That was the impetus for a lot of those characters. They all had unfinished business. They didn't get to play that one last song."

"It makes them wonder what life is all about?" I asked.

"Exactly, and I think it really put it into perspective. *We really need to focus on the important things. But this is our little way of telegraphing that to our loved ones: It's not lost on us. Even though we're not around, we recognize what is important.*"

The work began to take its toll on Aonuma, who felt the pressure of the project more than anyone. One night, after working on an in-game event featuring the Deku, Aonuma had a nightmare in which he was being chased around by a Deku and woke up screaming. The next morning, Aonuma went to work and, as he tells it, "that's when [Takumi] Kawagoe-san told me that he finished making a movie for the Dekus, so I had him show it to me... and that movie was exactly like my dream!"

As the year progressed, Miyamoto wound up calling more former members of the *Ocarina* team in to help finish *Majora*. "Once we realized that our initial setup just wasn't going to work, I was forced to recall the original team members," Miyamoto said in the Hobonichi interview. "In the end, around 70% of the team was made up of people who had worked on *Ocarina of Time*."

The one-year goal was going to be tight, and Aonuma often thought about how disappointed he'd be if they didn't make the deadline. Then, late in the game's development, Miyamoto mentioned that if Aonuma's team needed more time, they could always push back *Majora*'s release. "I got mad," Aonuma told Iwata. "I said to [Miyamoto], pretty loudly, 'There's no way we can do that now!'" Iwata thought that was pretty funny. You get the sense people don't often talk like that to Shigeru Miyamoto.

MAJORA THE OPEN TEXT

Everywhere you go in Termina, there is loss.

The inconsolable Goron Elder's son misses his father, who has been trapped in a block of ice. The ghost of Darmani misses being alive. The Zora Lulu misses her eggs. Pamela misses her cursed father. Tael misses Tatl. Link misses Navi. The Deku Butler misses his son "who left home long ago," he tells Link. "I wonder where he has gone…what he is doing… If only he would write me a letter." We later learn his son was killed by Skull Kid and turned into a tree. Some of these problems will be solved with heroics while others simply cannot.

"When I originally played *Majora's Mask* in 2000," Patrick Klepek writes in an article for Kotaku, "I was struck by how powerful I felt: I could weave through time, collect a gallery of masks, and defeat the largest monsters. Playing it fifteen years later, I'm struck more by how powerless Link truly is. He might save the world, but he can't rescue everyone along the way. We can't do that in our own lives, either."

It's no wonder fans applied the "Five Stages of Grief" model to *Majora*, pairing a game suffused with death to a grief model that has been popular for half a century.

When the Kübler-Ross "Five Stages of Grief" model came out in 1969, it was a massive hit that extended well beyond the bubble of psychologists and caretakers. The concept caught on with the general public like few psychological concepts ever do.

At the time, my dad was starting his career as a minister—a job largely spent counseling members of his congregation. "Those of us in ministry were just blown away by [Kübler-Ross]," he told me. By his account, everybody got a little too excited—himself included. "It's like, 'Oooh, now we understand grief.' And, 'Oh! Yes. Now I'm dealing with somebody. And they're at this stage! I can name it! I can pinpoint it!' I've got control of this process. And when they have another kind of response, I'm really tempted to say, 'You know what *that* is? That's stage 4.'" As my dad admits, part of the appeal of the model is that it takes the difficult, weighty subject of grief and tidies it up.

But anyone who's lost somebody can tell you that, in practice, actual grief is much messier than five sequential steps. We skip stages, repeat others, and invent new stages. Researchers who published their findings in the *Journal of the American Medical Association* found that most people who have lost someone skip Denial altogether, and that the most-reported feeling among the grieving was simply yearning for the lost person's company.

Kübler-Ross herself later regretted having presented the stages in such a linear way. At best, the model is a useful tool that gives people license to feel the pain of death, and to sense the normalcy of their own grief. At worst, it makes people feel as if they're grieving wrong.

Similarly, the model and *Majora's Mask* don't line up as neatly as theorists would have you believe. In her video "The Legend of Zelda Theory: The Five Stages of Grief," YouTuber VortexxyGaming asks, "If the Stages of Grief are all about a single person coming to terms with mortality, why would a game want to spread that grief out amongst many different characters?" To that I'd add: Why would some of those emotions, like the Deku King's anger over his kidnapped daughter, have nothing to do with death?

Still, the "Stages of Grief in *Majora*" theory had so much momentum that, in 2015, *Game Informer* finally laid out the evidence to Aonuma during an interview, asking, "Was [the Kübler -Ross model] considered during development, or is this just a fan interpretation?"

"It's certainly true that each one of these different episodes you talked about has a different emotional cast to it," Aonuma replied. "One feels like it's tinged with sadness, and another with anger—that certainly was intentional. But, I also want to point out that it's not that each one of these episodes only has the one emotion that they are conveying. There are certainly other notes that we're trying to hit as well."

In other words: Fans are correct that the developers intentionally created an emotionally dynamic game. But to arbitrarily match it to model five distinct responses does not enliven the game, it shrinks it down. It tosses out the many other emotions that arise both in the scenes mentioned and throughout the rest of the game.

To be clear, I don't mean to imply that this fan theory doesn't work simply because Aonuma says it doesn't. I think it doesn't work because he's right that there is more to this game than a quick and easy answer. We can look back on a theory that looked so plausible moments ago and can see that we made some leaps. We observed these vivid, universal emotions, and then, instead of appreciating them for what they are, we leapt to grab the nearest pop psychology framework.

What we now know about the Stages of Grief is that, while it is observant and useful to point to all these ways that people deal with loss, it's reductive to say that they follow one particular pattern. The problem with the "Stages of Grief in *Majora*" theory is the same problem that's been with the Kübler-Ross model all along.

•

If it annoys you that I'm using developer interviews to poke holes into a beloved fan theory, you may be happy to learn that much of literary criticism is on your side. In many ways, the debate over the "correct" reading of Zelda mirrors an old and often boring debate that's been going on in philosophy and academia for decades.

Literary theorists in the 1930s known as formalists believed everything you needed to know about a Zelda game was contained right there in the cartridge itself. You shouldn't have to know anything about the game's setting, the environment the game came out of, or the game's developer.

But there were problems with formalism. If I'm playing a game that draws from Japanese culture (as all Zelda games do), it might be useful to broaden our scope and look at the game through the lens of culture, as well as through other lenses such as psychology, politics, history, and (as if we humans could avoid it) personal experience. These lenses, taken together, were called reader-response criticism.

A Freudian reading could offer a psychological deep dive into Link's psyche—what's it like to have to save the world before you've ever been out on a date? A Marxist reading could look closely at Hyrulean power structures. A feminist reading could examine the series's spotty record of portraying Princess Zelda. A postcolonial reading might ask whether the Gerudo race's history of aggression against the Hylians might actually be a justified rebellion against their oppressors. In other words, we get to ask: What ways of seeing the game does the player herself bring to the table? How might her own experience and expertise be relevant to the discussion? The pitfall is that each of these lenses is so specific that it might not be a great fit for every game. Sometimes a magical rod is just a magical rod.

Later, literary theorists called the structuralists swooped in and said, "You know what's *really* useful? Breaking Zelda games down into their component parts to see what conclusions we can draw about humanity (or Hylianity) in general." And what the structuralists found was that we're all using symbols to make meaning all the time—not just with our words, but with our body language, our tones of voice, our eating habits, etc. "Ya know," the structuralists said, "you can read *anything* as a 'text'—a sword, a mask, a concert, a wedding." Everywhere you looked was meaning.

But all these theoretical models started making people nervous, and these people pointed out to the structuralists that art isn't a goddamn science. If you reduce a Zelda game to its component parts, you've murdered it. Meaning can't be plotted onto an axis—that's why

Robin Williams had the boys tear those pages out of their books in *Dead Poets Society*!

Furthermore, language itself is complex, nuanced, contradictory, and ever-changing. *Majora's Mask* naturally contains meaning that Aonuma and Koizumi did not themselves intend, even before it is translated from the original Japanese. Theorists like Jacques Derrida remind us, then, that the discovery of meaning is always going to be more journey than destination.

Just as every Zelda game is a reaction against the last Zelda game, every school of literary theory attempts to make up for the failures of the last.

To put my cards on the table, I believe that a mix of the above approaches is the best way to arrive at truth, just as multiple videos of the same crime reveal different details. Looking directly at *Majora* itself is worthwhile. Zooming way out to look at the whole series is worthwhile. Zooming way in on a single moment or word or rock is worthwhile. Bringing my own experience to the discussion is worthwhile. Reading up on how the game was made is worthwhile. Reading up on Japan in the year 2000 is worthwhile. Reading up on the discussion around the game is worthwhile.

In criticism, as in fandom, you're the adventurer here. What are you excited to dig into first?

•

As we've seen from stories of the game's creation, *Majora's Mask* was not built in the shadows by mischievous puzzlemakers attempting to imbue their game with hidden meaning. It was instead the product of very specific conditions: the *Ocarina* assets, some cool dungeon ideas, an aborted board game, a tense wedding, a strict deadline, a team of skilled developers working independently from one another, a unique level of trust from the bossman, the gift of a lack of expectations from fans, and the usual goal for any Zelda game—to make the game interesting, fun, and novel. How could Link be secretly dead? Or secretly dreaming? Or acting out the exact beats of a psychology fad? There was barely enough time for Link to be playable.

And yet I believe that our eager fan theorists are on to something, just as Alex Hall was on to something when he chose a haunted copy of *Majora* as the subject of his creepypasta instead of, say, a haunted copy of *Diddy Kong Racing*. That's because *Majora* is mysterious. *Majora* is interpretable. *Majora* is an open text.

A literary concept that has always been useful to me is Umberto Eco's distinction between an open text (or "open work"), which is a piece of art that allows for multiple interpretations from the reader, and a closed text, which communicates just one intended meaning.

"Some [TV] shows, there's not much room for the viewer to move within," David Lynch tells Jeff Jensen in an *Entertainment Weekly* interview about *Twin Peaks*. "It's a surface thing. You watch it, bang, you've got it. Then there are other shows where there might be things to wonder about."

Rage Against the Machine's self-titled debut album is a closed text. *Sgt. Pepper* is an open text. *The Devil Wears Prada* is a closed text. *The Shining* is an open text. *Law & Order: SVU* is a closed text. *The Leftovers* is an open text. *The Prince* is Machiavelli's famously blunt closed text. Akira Kurosawa's film *Rashomon* is a famously ambiguous open text. This book is a closed text—I'm aiming for clarity here. My first book, *Fun Camp*, is an open text—the novel guides you through the different perspectives of several narrators and ultimately does not side with any one of them.

Often, when young people first encounter open texts, their first instinct is to go in one of two directions. One is to come up with a single interpretation, defend it to the death, and argue that there is no openness at all to the diligent sleuth. The other direction is to pitch a fit at the idea of an open text at all—assuming that the author has either failed to communicate an intended point or is being deliberately malicious. "What was the point of that?" is a complaint I got about particular stories and poems the year I taught college literature. Flannery O'Connor's "A Good Man is Hard to Find," for instance, is a tightly-wound short story in which a family of dopes gets murdered by a serial killer. It's one of the coolest stories you'll ever find in an anthology, and it always, always gets some what-was-the-point-of-thats. The answers I gave were often deeply unsatisfying to my students: "I don't think what the author was doing can really be summed up in a single sentence." And: "Uhhhhhhhhh…" And: "What did *you* take from it?"

In her own time, O'Connor herself got sick of dealing with what-was-the-point-of-thats from readers. "It seems to be a paradox that the larger and more complex the personal view, the easier it is to compress it into fiction," she writes in her essay collection *Mystery and Manners*. "People have a habit of saying, 'What is the theme of your story?' and they expect you to give them a statement: 'The theme of my story is the economic pressure of the machine on the middle class'—or some such absurdity. And when they've got a statement like that, they go off happy and feel it is no longer necessary to read the story. Some people have the notion that you read the story and then climb out of it into the meaning, but for the fiction writer himself the whole story is the meaning, because it is an experience, not an abstraction."

I pick O'Connor here in part to show that this is a conversation that's been going on for a long time. The difference between when O'Connor was writing and now, though, is in the democratization of the internet. Instead of dealing only with the occasionally reductive review or letter to the editor, we now must contend with *anybody* who has an idea about what a work is trying to say. And in the age of Reddit and YouTube, unsound theories can build upon one another until "the body of *Majora's Mask* criticism" begins to look like a teetering tower bound for ruin—kind of like the very Tower of Babel that some theorists believe *Majora* is an allegory about.

Aonuma, for his part, gets a little tired of this line of questioning too. He spends all this time building an experience like, for instance, *A Link Between Worlds*, and the burning question all these fans and interviewers want to ask him about is how it's possible in the Zelda timeline that Majora's Mask is hanging on Link's wall. *What does this mean for Hyrule, Mr. Aonuma?* The answer: He thought it'd be a fun cameo.

Far more often, though, it's not what-was-the-point-of-thats Aonuma has faced but instead questions that amount to "Will you confirm my pet theory and make it canon?" In many ways, these two responses are opposites: One person refuses to do the work of interpreting while the other interprets obsessively. To me, what both approaches share is the impulse to take a work teeming with meaning and attempt to reduce it down to something so easy to digest that the work itself no longer matters.

In her landmark 1964 essay, "Against Interpretation," Susan Sontag rails against the thematic algebra of reading a book and then saying, "Look, don't you see that X is really—or, really means—A? That Y is really B? That Z is really C?"

"Interpretation is the revenge of the intellect upon art," she continues. "Even more. It is the revenge of the intellect upon the world. To interpret is to impoverish, to deplete the world—in order to set up a shadow world of 'meanings.'"

At the time of her writing, literary criticism was still in the midst of its love affair with the reader-response criticism of Marxist and especially Freudian readings, an act which Sontag saw as turning "all observable phenomena" into fodder to "be probed and pushed aside to find the true meaning—the latent content—beneath." Despite her chainsaw of a title, Sontag was never truly against interpretation, but was rather against the sort of interpretation that "solves" a book in a single sentence: the sort of interpretation that closes the open.

My dad's introduction to open texts was not Umberto Eco or Flannery O'Connor but instead reading interviews with Paul Simon. "*What does that line mean in 'The Boxer'?*" my dad said in the voice of an imagined interviewer. "*Come on, Paul. It's been out there for 40 years. Now you can spill the beans.* And Simon says something like, 'You know, there are lines in a lot of my biggest, most popular songs where I just liked the way they sounded. Or it just needed to rhyme.'" To *American Songwriter* in 2011, for instance, Simon likened the songwriting process to "wandering down a path and you don't know what the destination is."

"Any time there's a creator," my dad continued, "I have to remember, 'Don't assume there's one right answer.'"

It's normal to resist open texts. Our brains are categorizing, labeling, ranking, stereotyping machines constantly tasked with turning chaos into order. "Order makes it easier to be a person, to navigate this sloppy world," writes *You Are Not So Smart* author David McRaney. "Pattern recognition leads to food, protects you from harm. You are born looking for clusters where chance events have built up like sand into dunes. You are able to read these words because your ancestors recognized patterns and changed their behavior to better acquire food and avoid becoming it." Responding to an open text with "What was the point of that?" can be another way of saying, "I don't have time for this artsy horseshit! I'm just trying to survive out here!"

But then eventually you may fall for a work of art whose meaning you can't quite put your finger on, and so you fill in some of the gaps with your own interpretation, and you find that you *like* being asked to bring your own interpretation to the party. Not all the time. Sometimes you want to crank up the car stereo and shout, "Fuck you, I won't do whatcha tell me," over and over. But as you get used to flexing your interpretive muscles, you begin to recognize that open texts are not challenges to overcome or puzzle boxes to unlock, they are friendly invitations. They are works of art that hand you the controller.

CULTURAL DISTANCE

ON JULY 2, 2000, the American *Nintendo Power* writer Jason Leung flew to Japan for the first time ever. Having only recently been named the English localization director for *Majora's Mask*, Leung was to spend the next few weeks working directly with the *Majora* team at Nintendo's home base of Nintendo Co., Ltd. (NCL) in Kyoto. Upon arriving to NCL for the first time, Leung looked up at the drab gray compound and thought, *This is it?*

The inside fared no better. Most employees wore lab coats. Everybody did morning calisthenics together in front of the building. And at lunch, the employees would eat at long tables together in a cafeteria. It reminded Leung of a private school with uniforms.

"[NCL] looks like a cross between a hospital and an old school building," Leung wrote in a diary entry for Nintendo.com. "Not that I was expecting circus animals or anything, but NCL appears sort of sterile. I'm beginning to wonder where all that creativity comes from…" Nintendo had asked Leung to keep an online diary that was released to the site and later excerpted in the pages of *Nintendo Power*. This was a rare peek behind the curtain in 2000, back when the gaming public knew much less about localization.

Today, Leung works in film and TV development at Disney, and we met at a Burbank coffee shop near his office one weekday afternoon. Friendly and easy to talk to, Leung looked like he could be my age, although math tells me he's at least fifteen years older.

Leung first came to work at Nintendo in 1996 after seeing an ad for the job in *Seattle Weekly*, and he was hired to work on both *Nintendo Power* and the official strategy guides that were big business at the time. As a writer and a video game fan, it was a dream job for Leung on two fronts. Like many writers, Leung is more of a story guy than a mechanics guy—which made him a great fit for work as a localizer.

His first shot at localization came with a much less challenging game: *Yoshi's Story*, also for the N64. As Leung and his *Nintendo Power* colleagues played through a ROM of the forthcoming game to create the player's guide, they noticed that the English text was a little off. "And the person who was localizing it, he was—nothing against him—but I think he wasn't putting as much into it as he should've been," Leung said. So one of the higher-ups, Yoshio Tsuboike, suggested that Leung and two other *Nintendo Power* writers divvy up the text and do a rewrite.

Before *Majora*'s development, the Zelda series from *A Link to the Past* through *Ocarina* was localized by Dan Owsen. When Owsen was in Kyoto working on *Ocarina*, Leung was in Seattle playing the ROM and working on the official *Ocarina* strategy guide. "I'd be playing the early version," Leung told me, "seeing his text fill in and then I would tell him, 'That seems kinda out of place,' or that kind of thing."

"I remember getting kinda hung up on him using the word 'scuba' in *Ocarina*," Leung said. "There's a diving challenge, and SCUBA [is an acronym for] self-contained underwater breathing apparatus, so that term doesn't make sense in that context." So when Owsen moved on to managing Nintendo.com, it made sense that Leung was the one to fill his shoes. Leung's boss, Leslie Swan, recommended him for the gig. This was to be a much bigger assignment than *Yoshi's Story*.

However, the text first had to be translated into English by Bill Trinen—a huge job. "*Majora's Mask* was not so hard," Trinen told *Game Informer* in 2003, "but all the relationships with the characters in the game and all the different times of day […] and trying to keep everything straight mentally as you're going through the translation was a pretty big challenge. That was also in an extremely difficult and tight deadline—I missed

E3 that year because I had to stay back at NOA and translate *Majora's Mask*."

Once Trinen's text was ready, Leung was pulled from his work at *Nintendo Power* for four months and given a laptop containing all of Trinen's translated text in a giant color-coded Excel spreadsheet.

Leung also got a ROM of the game so he could play alongside Trinen's translation. "I thought [*Majora*] was amazing, and really difficult, and I'd never seen anything like it before. But the challenge was I was playing it as I was writing the text, so there were a lot of parts where I was writing but I hadn't played it yet."

Bill Trinen had made *Majora*'s text accurate. Leung's job was to make it fun: "to polish it, make it more conversational, and add different tonalities to the characters," Leung said. For instance, it was important that the characters not sound too similar to one another—that some sound more or less formal, that others have little vocal tics "like the Goron who'd say 'goro' after everything."

Through the years since his work on *Majora*, Leung has been happy to see how English-speaking fans have taken to his work, sharing favorite quotes from the game. No line of his is more famous than the one the Happy Mask Salesman tells Link on their first meeting, and again every time the world ends: "You've met with a terrible fate, haven't you?"

There are a hundred ways you could communicate the line's meaning: "Your destiny is dark indeed, isn't it?" Or: "You're fated to experience awful things, aren't you?" Or: "Bad stuff is coming your way, am I right?" But the version Leung came up with is concise, clear, poetic, and lightly archaic in a way that nicely amps up the mystery of the Happy Mask Salesman—making him feel like a man out of time. To me, it's the use of "met with" that takes the line to the next level. It sounds as if predestination is a mysterious stranger you've crossed paths with on a solitary road, and that just maybe this terrible fate could be reversed. There was nothing inevitable about the way Leung chose to phrase the line—an example of how localization is more art than science.

Leung also looked for opportunities to lighten things up wherever he could. When you meet the jugglers in Clock Town, they tell a corny joke that was all Leung: "Did you hear about the kidnapping?" "Oh, my! The kidnapping?" "Yep! But then the kid woke up. Get it? Kid napping? Hoo…I got a million of 'em!"

"There was no joke in [the original text]," Leung explained. "They were saying, 'The world's gonna end, but we're still juggling, trying to entertain.' So I took that a step further."

A favorite detail from my conversation with Leung was the confirmation that he'd knowingly worked in a reference to a TLC song: Early in the game, when you are still a Deku Scrub, the bombers won't let you into their secret society. They tell you: "No scrubs!"

Leung began his work in the United States, smoothing out and stylizing the roughly translated text. "For pretty much seven days a week, fifteen or more hours a day," he wrote in his diary, "I've been trying to finish this game and rewrite its 8,000 or so script pieces (ranging from single sentences to long paragraphs)."

Leung had to get the work done on time because soon he'd be flying to Kyoto to work directly with the team there. "I had been working [hard]," Leung told me. "I would take that laptop home with me every weekend […] and every day, and then at night—you could see how long that document was—and I was like, 'I've got to churn through all of this.'" During his long weeks in Termina, Leung felt a new appreciation for the *Majora* characters who worked too hard and missed their families.

•

Two days after Leung's arrival in Kyoto, *Majora*'s script director Mitsuhiro Takano returned home to Japan from his honeymoon, and—with the help of interpreter Masashi Goto—the two got to work. Takano and Leung spent long days in a boardroom with a laptop and a whiteboard, going over the script line by line to make sure that it squared up with the original text.

For instance, Leung had accidentally included the word "aunt" in the English version, when the Japanese word for "aunt" had in context meant its synonym— simply "a middle-aged woman." "Luckily, we caught the mistake," wrote Leung, "so now the mayor's wife isn't already related to her future daughter-in-law."

The naming of the Zora band also presented a challenge. The band's original Japanese name translated to "Blue Swamp," which in Japanese sounds similar to "Aonuma." "So they thought that was a fun pun, but it didn't sound like a catchy band name in English," Leung said. He and his colleagues would try to come up with new names and found it was as difficult as agreeing on a real band name. "I'd be sitting in the room coming up with text, and I'd say, 'How about *this*,' and [Goto] would run it by everybody, and they'd say, 'I dunno…'" Finally, the suggestion Indigo-Go's made all of them laugh.

"Because of the Indigo Girls?" I guessed.

"No," Leung said. "It was playing off the Go-Go's and then the color. I wanted to stick with blue since they're a Zora band. But I do remember coming across articles where people thought it was a cross between the Indigo Girls and the Go-Go's."

"Your Lilith Fair fans are so disappointed!" I said.

"Yeah," Leung deadpanned, "but there's a lot of Sarah McLachlan quotes in the game."

Working so closely with Mitsuhiro Takano gave Leung the impression that Takano is one of the undersung heroes of *Majora*'s development. After all, he was responsible for most of the actual text and dialogue in the game, and also had a role in creating many characters. When Aonuma and Miyamoto brought Takano on board, he was fresh from writing the fully-voiced dialogue for *Star Fox 64* and had also recently served as co-director of the popular N64 game *1080° Snowboarding*.

The three-man team was sometimes visited in their boardroom by Aonuma, Miyamoto, and Takashi Tezuka—the *Link's Awakening* director who worked on *Majora* as a supervisor. Every now and then, Miyamoto would try out ideas on Leung, Takano, and Goto that had nothing to do with *Majora*—like what to call the game console that was to follow the N64.

"[Miyamoto] would come in every so often and say, 'What do you think about this name?'" Leung told me. "The names were all different versions of Something Cube. And the frontrunner for him was JoyCube. I kept saying, 'That doesn't sound right for a game console…'"

"Yeah," I offered, "it sounds like a sex robot."

Leung pushed back on the JoyCube name as best he could. "Contextually, I understand what you're going for," he told Miyamoto, "but in America we don't use that word a lot. That's not gonna go over well with the game community."[6]

Leung was catching the *Majora* team at an interesting moment. The game had been out in Japan since April, but work was far from finished. The version of *Majora* that first shipped in Japan had a lot of bugs, so they were fixing them one by one. Japanese players complained about the lack of save points, too, and so the team was working to add them into the game.

"We had six months in between [the Japanese and English versions]," Leung said. "Usually, things are done almost simultaneously. This one, we had the luxury of learning what the Japanese fans had issues with. So a lot of [those changes] were coming through while I was still in Redmond playing the early ROM."

One day, Aonuma and Takano took the time to map out Majora's entire story for Leung, going so far as to diagram the storylines of and relationships between each of the inhabitants of Clock Town. "A giant Venn diagram," Leung said. "*This is how this impacts this, and this is how these people's lives overlap.* Things like that. And that really helps because when I'm localizing, everything's

6 Miyamoto would finally get his way in 2017 when the Nintendo Switch's detachable controller, the Joy-Con, was released.

linear—but when you see it that way, it's like, *Ooooh, okay. I see how this dialogue will evolve.*"

Leung was tasked with writing dozens of replies for each character depending on which mask Link is wearing (if he wears one at all) and when the dialogue falls on the three-day timeline. "My big wish is that players will talk to every character on all three days, wearing all 24 masks," Leung wrote in his diary. "That way, the tons of dialogue and little jokes I wrote for each situation won't go unread. Chances are, though, most people won't see more than two-thirds of the dialogue that was scripted for the game. Sigh."

During my own playthrough, I thought of Leung's comment when I visited the owner of the swordsman's school in Clock Town, and he wouldn't let me train because I was wearing my Bunny Hood. "Ahem…" he said, "if you study the way of the sword here, you'll get your bunny ears dirty, so put them away."

So, out of curiosity, I tried out every mask I had so far to see exactly how the swordsman would ask me to take my mask off. Sure enough, each reply was unique: When I wore the Goron Mask, he sucked up to me. When I wore the Deku Mask, he talked down to me. When I wore the Bomb Mask, the swordsman was offended that I'd bring "such an evil weapon" into his "training center for teaching the sacred sword." When I wore the Great Fairy Mask, he flirted with me:

"I'll lose my focus if I try to instruct you while you're wearing that. Leave it at home. Or... I could keep it for you." And when I wore the Mask of Scents, he took my piglike appearance as a dig on his own hygiene: "I am not stinky! I take a bath at least once a month!" You could play through the game several times and still never read most of those replies.

Leung's English version was to be used as the basis for the French, German, and Spanish editions of the game. After he'd been in Japan for two weeks, the other localizers arrived—and suddenly Leung went from the fish out of water to the resident *Majora* expert.

Since most of NCL was not fluent in English, it was his interpreter, Goto, who Leung got to know best. As they worked on the Japanese-to-English localization of *Majora*, Goto was also working on the English-to-Japanese localization of *Perfect Dark*. Back home, Leung had already worked on the Player's Guide for *Perfect Dark*, so he was able to advise Goto.

Because Leung and Goto were always together, both wore glasses, and had a similar sense of style, Aonuma and the team began referring to Leung and Goto as "the brothers." At first, Leung needed Goto to interpret their joke, but it happened often enough that Leung memorized the word. "I remember the final photo we took before I left," Leung said. The men called Goto and Leung "the brothers" again, and Leung finally got the joke on his own. "And then they went, 'Oh my god, you understand us now!'"

When Leung flew home to Seattle, he immediately resumed his post at *Nintendo Power*, but was he not done with the game yet. *Majora's Mask* needed a player's guide now, and there was nobody better equipped to write it than him.

•

It's easy to forget while playing a cohesive game just how collaborative the art form is. In the case of *Majora*, creators made unilateral decisions, often without asking one another for permission. An example from the English version is Leung's reference to TLC's "No Scrubs." It's in there. It's officially part of the game. Does it "not count" because Aonuma and Koizumi didn't come up with it? From what I can tell, they didn't come up with most of the lines in the game either—that was Takano's job. When the "voice" of a game is decentralized, as it is in just about all big games, questions of authorial intent become thornier.

In a 2015 interview with Aonuma, GameSpot began a question by prefacing it with an almost-apology: "The fans probably think about the Zelda timeline a lot more than you do as creators. I imagine that when you were putting together *Majora's Mask*, you were mostly just trying to make a fun experience that was a follow-up to

Ocarina and that used some of those same assets." And then the interviewer still went on to ask, "[H]ow does *Majora's Mask* fit into the world of Hyrule? Especially since it does use so many characters who are familiar but at the same time a little bit strange?"

Aonuma replied, "It's difficult to talk about how Termina fits into the world of Hyrule because it's almost like it's another dimension. When I think about the very beginning of *Majora's Mask*, I like to think about the characters as already being in Termina at that point.

But honestly, I don't know that we thought about it in exactly those terms at the very beginning of development of this game. Our goal, rather, was to create something familiar that has been warped in a very unusual and interesting way."

When I interviewed Jason Leung, I asked for his take on the game's many fan theories.

"I've looked into it over the past couple weeks, just preparing for this [conversation]," he said. "A lot of those, it's like any kind of fan theory—that's all it is. It's not really what was intended. But I think it's great that they're digging deeper to find some meaning in it. There was one that was very much about religion and the Tower of Babel. And they were really focusing on a lot of Western culture."

Many of the *Majora* fan theories I've found have that in common. The Tower of Babel is from the Torah.

Purgatory before Heaven is a Catholic concept. The Greeks founded Western philosophy, not Eastern philosophy. And Elisabeth Kübler-Ross grew up in Switzerland and lived, for her entire career, in the United States. Her ideas did not catch fire in Asia the way they did for us.

Leung is not the only one to pick up on how we tend to read Japanese games with Western eyes. "Books like *The Legend of Zelda and Theology* and *The Legend of Zelda and Philosophy: I Link Therefore I Am* […] are predominantly Western in their thought," writes Sterling Anderson Osborne in his master's thesis, *Linking Masks with Majora: The Legend of Zelda: Majora's Mask and Noh Theater*. He quotes from the *Zelda and Theology* anthology, which states outright that the articles in the book exist to "clarify and provide you with a better understanding of why [we] Christians believe what we believe." Which is to say, the book is forcing Zelda into its own Christian framework instead of attempting to meet the game where it is.[7]

Often, these made-up Western influences distract us from recognizing the actual influences that were right in

---

7 To be clear, *Zelda and Theology* understands that it's doing this and owns up to it. The book does not pretend that Zelda games are fundamentally religious texts, but rather uses these heroic fantasy stories for their metaphoric potential. In this way, *Zelda and Theology* displays more self-awareness than many fan theories do.

front of the game's creators. When Leung was in Kyoto, he saw influences on Nintendo games everywhere he went. "I made a point to go to the temples to see all the things Mr. Miyamoto had always talked about that inspired him as a kid—running around in the forest, exploring caves, and seeing temples. You see all of that stuff, and it's like, 'Okay, that's physically real.' You see Triforce symbols, you see masks, you see all these columns and all this architecture that looks just like what you see in these games." Leung offered the Keaton (fox) Mask as an example. "The fox is a popular animal in Shinto religions. Masks are a significant part of [Japanese] culture."

"It was nuts when I was walking around," he continued. "*Oh my god! That was in Star Fox!* Or: *That was in Mario!* You'd see little references. Mr. Miyamoto is just filing away every little thing and reusing it."

"I can pretty confidently say," Leung told me, "that what was the basis for *Majora's Mask* was really their own culture, and their own work and life experience."

Miyamoto, Aonuma, and Koizumi were pulling from whatever was around them—just like we Westerners naturally do when we set out to interpret their game through our own cultural lens. It's just that we're doing our interpreting from 6,000 miles away.

MAJORA'S EVOLVING
LEGACY

IN A DESERT MILITARY BASE, a white teenage boy plays *Majora's Mask* on a big TV. Cut to the rest of the world— the city, the desert, the suburbs—where everyone is watching him play on a live feed as an orange, faceless moon hovers ominously in the night sky. As the moon gets closer, people flee for their lives—and there's a quick single shot of several big scary dogs racing through the city streets. The minute-long commercial is free of talk until the final seconds, when an announcer says, "72 hours. One hope." And then comes the onscreen text: "THE WORLD IS WAITING ON YOU."

The TV commercial described above implies that the "three days 'til the moon kills us" plot of *Majora* is actually happening on Earth, and that our only hope for salvation is for you, the tireless gamer, to buy and complete the game. Dark, foreboding, contemporary, and urban, it's the least Zelda ad for Zelda I've ever seen. When the announcer soberly mentions that the game is "Rated E for Everyone," the question we consumers found ourselves asking was, "Should it be?"

The commercial was the centerpiece of a guerrilla marketing campaign that otherwise took place entirely on the internet. Web marketing at this time was considered important but mysterious. Big brands didn't pump huge money into the internet the way they soon would, but instead treated the potential to go viral (itself a recent concept) as a lotto you had to be in to win. It was only four years earlier in 1996 that, after seeing a poster for the upcoming movie *Independence Day*, I went home to the family computer, booted up Erol's Internet, and typed www.id4.com into the browser because, wow, this "blow up the White House" movie had *its own website*. Now, in 2000, it was assumed that the new Zelda game would have some sort of web presence, though what that presence would be was far less standardized than it is today. To their credit, Nintendo of America had fun with it.

The campaign mostly played itself out on two web-sites, radiozelda.com and z-science.com, across several weeks in real time. The two sites used a news feed format to elaborate on the story that was hinted at in the commercial, a story that goes like this.

A science organization called JRAMOA (an anagram I'll let you decipher) has discovered a parallel universe in which the moon is about to crash into Earth. "You might not like what you're about to hear," Radio Zelda warns us, "but this parallel universe is connected to our own universe. If something happens there, it happens here too." The projected date of the crash? October 26, 2000: *Majora*'s North American release date.

JRAMOA discovers that hope lies in a savior called The One[8] and begins a quest to find the only person on Earth who could save us all. Finalists include Canadian jewelry-maker Mindy Somaltro, Slovakian skier Alexandra Macozsek, and Indian scuba instructor Mahi Valandi. Most distressing is a Frenchman named Joseph Renaudierre who was basically kidnapped. "He fled south to Pamplona, Spain, but JRAMOA volunteers were able to take custody of him shortly thereafter," his bio says. "Though currently uncooperative, we can only hope that he quickly recognizes his obligation to aid the people of Earth."

Despite the diverse cast of candidates, JRAMOA eventually identifies The One as seventeen-year-old American Bryce Wilson—the same boy who appears in the dystopian commercial. Bryce happens to perfectly embody the cool skater archetype that appears in every video game commercial of this era.

A JRAMOA engineer explains, "Not only does Bryce have the proper genetic code, but he demonstrates nearly perfect performance in all applicable skill evaluations. His keen eyesight, extreme patience, and superb hand-eye coordination made him an obvious choice." To summarize,

---

8 Please note that *The Matrix* came out the previous year.

what we know so far about JRAMOA is that they kidnap people, they seem to like eugenics, and they believe we should put all our trust in a lone white savior: Uh-oh.

Luckily, *just* before JRAMOA goes Full Nazi, the story takes a fun turn: "[T]he exact nature of the equipment which Bryce Wilson will use to interact with the parallel universe" is revealed. It's not the "Charged-Coupled Device or Theometric Dishelver" originally assumed. "Dr. Rugeshi surprised many members of the scientific community when he announced that Bryce's interface would consist solely of a Nintendo 64 and a copy of the upcoming video game *The Legend of Zelda: Majora's Mask*." That's right, kids: His Nintendo skills are going to save the world. *And someday yours might too.* This plot twist is a meta marketing coup: Not only are we in a world in which a *Majora* doomsday situation is happening, but it is also a world in which *Majora* exists as a video game—and is our only hope for salvation.

Meanwhile, the world is built out with surprising panache in a campaign of fringe satellite websites that have the vibe of a couple of young NOA employees making each other laugh with little oversight.

Over at binkypinkerson.com, a doomsday prepper with capitalist motives sells urban survivalist courses such as "Decorating Ideas & Winning Barb-Wire Treatments for the Sophisticated Urban Survivor." "Did you know," asks Binky, "that a typical IKEA futon and a pack of tea candles can be easily converted into a makeshift flamethrower?"

At theendtimes.net, an eccentric religious couple named Patrick and Meg O'Connell seem happy that, unlike the twelve other apocalypses they predicted, this one is going to stick. To the haters, the O'Connells suggest you "be sure and send us a postcard from your extended vacation in the LAKE OF FIRE!!!"

At cryptochronology.org, KFC night shift worker and 12th-year grad student Jeremy Hogarth offers a historical deep dive in an attempt to explain the eschatological significance of the Mask of El Jhomara (another acronym + a stray "h") —which happens to look exactly like Majora's Mask. He connects the mask to the Sphinx, the Knights Templar, the Freemasons, the Illuminati, the Beatles' "I Am the Walrus," and the faked moon landing. Which is to say that, many years before our *Majora's Mask* fan theories existed, Nintendo was satirizing our *Majora's Mask* fan theories.[9]

The posts stop the day before the apocalypse, which was also the day before the North American release of *Majora*. "The One has been playing *Majora's Mask* extremely well," says Radio Zelda's final report, "but at this point it looks like it's gonna be close."

---

9   They were also roasting our collective furor in anticipation of the Y2K computer bug, which only months before had made everybody feel a little silly when it turned out to not be a big deal.

We never do learn the results. All the sites were abandoned, and within a couple years would redirect to nintendo.com. A few years after that, Nintendo stopped payment on the URLs altogether. But we're still all here, so we can only assume Bryce Wilson has succeeded. Perhaps, like Link, he was too humble to bask in our praise, and simply departed on his horse in search of a lost friend.

•

Scattered across the web is further evidence of Nintendo of America's ambitious $12 million promotional campaign for *Majora's Mask*. There's a VHS infomercial that played in-store at the many Toys 'R' Us locations that were, in the year 2000, still thriving. "Some consider it a sequel to the greatest video game ever," says the professionally enthused announcer. "Others claim that it's much better than the original!" "You could label it a sequel," says a young stoner-looking guy from Nintendo, "but then you'd have to take everything you know about sequels and throw it out the window." The ad strongly underscores the fact that those who pre-order are guaranteed a special edition gold cartridge with a "3D" holographic label.

Majora had Nintendo's full support—not just in its ads, but also in the pages of *Nintendo Power*. The game got coverage in three issues leading up to the game's release: In issue #132, it got a full-page preview. In #134, there's a five-page feature calling *Majora* "the most innovative adventure game of all time," featuring an interview with Aonuma, Miyamoto, and Tezuka. Then, in #136, there's the four-page diary of Jason Leung's trip to Japan to work.

And then came issue #137, featuring *Majora's Mask* on the cover. "It's not just a sequel," says the magazine's 9.4/10 review, "It's another legend in disguise." The review calls *Majora* "a deep and original experience" with a story that is "perhaps the strongest in the series." Elsewhere, *Nintendo Power* calls it "one of the most engrossing games I've ever played."

In the rest of the gaming press, the response was just as enthusiastic. "There's just so many subtle touches and intricacies that it boggles the mind," wrote IGN's Fran Mirabella III in his 9.9/10 review. Darren Zenko of *The Edmonton Journal* believed *Majora* was not just the best Zelda, but also the best N64 game. "Believe me when I tell you, it does not get any better than this." "What consistently bowls me over here is the profoundly artistic eye with which the game has been assembled," wrote Peter Olafson and Charles Herold in the *New York Times*. Greg Howson in the *Guardian* called the game "another Zelda triumph."

These reviews mostly praise the game's surface elements—fun dungeons, cool bosses, nice graphics—and the innovation of the three-day system and transformation masks. Nobody was digging as much into the game's emotional depth or atmosphere. Only GameSpot's 8.3/10 review was a bit less rapturous than the others. "Some will appreciate the game's differences, while others will find the game's focus on minigames and side quests tedious and slightly out of place," writes the author—presumably filing the game's Clock Town missions under "side quests."

But that's a good example of the way the response to *Majora's* has changed over time. Even among people who loved the game, it's clear that players in 2000 and 2020 are latching on to very different elements. Back then, this game was the height of Zelda adventuring. Today, it's the height of heart.

•

Majora's Mask was the 12th best-selling game on the system—and, pivotally, it came out later than any of the eleven games that outperformed it. Sales numbers were reported at 3.36 million copies sold, not including future releases on the Wii and Wii U's Virtual Console service. That's a little under half the sales of *Ocarina*, a game that took a bigger staff around three times as long to make.

The sales numbers are more impressive when you consider all that was stacked against the game.

"This was end of the life cycle for N64," Leung told me. "Nobody was really expecting a Zelda game. They all knew about 'the Dolphin.'[10] So everybody was just

10 The Dolphin was the codename for the forthcoming GameCube.

waiting for, okay, there's gonna be a new Mario, so what is that gonna be?" Leung never got the impression that Nintendo was disappointed that *Majora* did not sell at *Ocarina* numbers. "In the end, a Zelda game is a Zelda game. And if you give it the attention, those people who did get it [will] care about it."

The next problem was that the game required an Expansion Pak, which was a small cartridge that doubled the N64's available 4MB of RAM. You installed the Pak by removing the system's original "Jumper Pak" cartridge and replacing it with the new one. It was an attempt to breathe a little new life into a dying console, and it was a marketing ploy that totally worked on young Gabe. My copy of *Donkey Kong 64* came bundled with the Pak, complete with copy boasting about the "enhanced graphics" now possible because of the upgrade. I eventually fell for the marketing of *Perfect Dark* (which required the Pak for the game's main content) and bought that game too. It was only years later that I learned the real reason *DK64* came bundled with the Pak: The game contained a game-breaking bug that caused *DK64* to crash—but when you doubled the RAM, it took many hours for the bug to surface, and it was rare for anyone to play long enough to encounter it. Nintendo had crunched the numbers and found it was better to offer a free Expansion Pak with every game and get *DK64* out in time for the holidays than to take the time to fix the bug.

While other games on the N64 benefited slightly from its expanded RAM, *Majora* was the only other game in the system's lifespan that *required* the Expansion Pak. This became part of the hype in the game's promotional campaign: The Pak allowed for better textures and more onscreen models than *Ocarina*, and got rid of the pesky fog that *Ocarina* had to employ to fudge its long-distance rendering. This was, by a slim margin, the Graphically Superior Zelda Game.

But for gamers who did not go in for *Donkey Kong 64*, could the Pak have been a major deterrent to buying *Majora*? According to IGN's Levi Buchanan, the unbundled Pak sold for $50 on its 1998 release. Although that price eventually came down, there were reports that when *Majora* released in 2000, many stores had plenty of copies of the game but not enough copies of the required Expansion Pak. The high price and the Pak's limited availability was likely a huge deterrent.

Finally, *Majora* had to compete with the fact that the game shared its launch date with the PlayStation 2. And the game competed with not just the PS2 hardware, but also (I'm gonna go ahead and call it) the greatest lineup of Day One launch titles in video game history, featuring brand new games in hit franchises such as Madden, NHL, Ridge Racer, Street Fighter, Tekken, Dead or Alive, Ready 2 Rumble, Dynasty Warriors, Armored Core, and Rayman. It also introduced the soon-to-be-popular franchises of SSX and Unreal Tournament. All on the same day. The gaming press can be forgiven for letting an N64 game get a little lost in the shuffle.

•

When I asked Jason Leung whether he felt fans understood the quality of *Majora's Mask* immediately or it took years for them to come around, he described it as a combination of the two. "It was definitely rewarding to see people liking it, but it was a very divisive game when it first came out because a lot of people wanted just another Zelda game."

"Immediately after [the release]," he continued, "I just felt like it kinda… happened. People liked it. A lot of people bought the limited [edition holographic] cart. And those are the Zelda fans who will buy whatever. But then it was just a Zelda game. The GameCube came out, and *Mario Sunshine*, and all that other stuff. Everybody was quick to move on to the next thing."

I mentioned that, before the game's release, fans had grumbled that this huge game *only* had four dungeons.

"A lot of people judged it on that, thinking 'That's such a tiny game,' and it's not until you start playing it that you really understand. That was the barrier they had to get past. They thought it was just a tiny version of *Ocarina*."

"There's a learning curve," I said. "And the learning curve involves watching the world die in a fiery hell."

"You have to let [the end of the world] happen that one time," Leung said. "And that's tough, and you feel like, 'Now I've got to do it all over again.' Back then, I remember trying to tell a lot of my friends, 'No, you have to play through this whole thing—you will really get it. I'm not just telling you this because I want you to read everything I wrote. This is an amazing game.' […] A lot of the reviews were really good, but I think for the general public, it was an easy game to write off. So a lot of the fandom came up later."

The decade that followed was kind to *Majora*. Players who'd put the game down as kids would come back to it years later and this time really get it—and then head online to talk to fellow fans. Year after year, *Majora's* fandom continued to grow as the game saw ports to GameCube, Wii, and Wii U, and as N64 emulators improved.

The moment Leung understood how much public opinion had shifted was when GameFAQs called *Majora* the Game of the Decade in 2010, beating *Super Smash Bros. Brawl* in the final round of a fan-voted bracket tournament. "That meant so much to me because it meant that people do get it," Leung said.

•

Even as fans noticed the depth of *Majora's* themes on closer inspection, other aspects of the game were clunky in a way that only got more apparent over time as 3D games continued to improve.

Majora's Mask is a hard game, though not in the sense that it's much of a test of your reflexes, resource management, or battle strategy. This isn't *Dark Souls*. *Majora*, like a lot of games of the N64/PS1 era, is "What am I supposed to do next?" hard. Diehards would say the game doesn't believe in handholding, and would accuse you of being the type of gamer who *liked* Navi's incessant shouts in *Ocarina*. I'd be more inclined to say that *Majora*'s greatest weakness is that it fails at the sort of useful environmental signposting that shows the player how the game works. If you're playing the original N64 version, using a player's guide or looking up tips online is the only way you're going to beat *Majora* without sinking dozens of hours into trial and error. The original Japanese version of *Majora* is especially cruel: It contains no save points, and instead only saves your game when you start a new three-day cycle.

In interviews, Aonuma has waffled somewhat on how he feels about the game's "difficult" reputation. He told *Game Informer* that when *Majora* came out, the internet was young enough that he didn't hear from players the way he does now, but he "certainly did have a lot of opportunities to talk to friends and family." He continued that "someone mentioned that they got pretty close to throwing the controller at one point, and that really stuck with me."

Other times, Aonuma shows an iconoclastic pride for having made a game to be wrestled with. Onstage at a concert performance of the game's music, Aonuma praised the game's difficulty: "Many games have a shorthand—a set of unspoken rules that they share. But *Majora's Mask* breaks those rules."

In conversation with Iwata, Aonuma even credits the game's challenge as the primary appeal that keeps players coming back to this entry. "It's all a challenge to our players. It's like we're saying to them, "Can you clear this?""

"It shifted from hospitality to a challenge," Iwata offers, and then recalls that when he first played the game, "it was like the game itself was screaming out to me, questioning me whether I had the dedication to play forward."

"That's because we didn't put in any kind of elements where we show people how to play this game," Aonuma replies. "The game was made for those who have played *Ocarina of Time*, so I felt like there wasn't a need for step-by-step instructions." And Aonuma says in several interviews that the team imagined an older audience for *Majora* than they had for *Ocarina*.

Even people who have played *Ocarina*, though, will often get stuck. For example, after you become a Goron, you have to find the Goron village elder and unthaw him. But unless you have spoken to his crying son first, it won't work. And then after you unthaw the Goron elder with Hot Springwater, you have to know to talk to him twice for him to teach you the half-song that allows the Goron son to teach you the rest. Clumsy chat quests like this may be "challenging," but they aren't rewarding. Unless you think like a Nintendo developer, you're better off looking it up online.

•

One day in 2012 or 2013, Miyamoto came knocking on Aonuma's door: It was time to put out a remastered version of *Majora's Mask* on 3DS.

"I think Miyamoto-san feels quite strongly that there are quite a lot of people [...] who gave up on the Nintendo 64 version partway through the journey," Aonuma told Iwata. "He probably felt that it was such a shame how we put so much in the game, but then people weren't able to see it all because they weren't able to get there." Finally, over a decade later, Miyamoto was upending the tea table. The prospect made Aonuma nervous. He didn't want to return to the game after so long for fear of what he'd see.

When Aonuma did jump back into Termina, he immediately began to make notes on what to change. For the first time, Aonuma played *Majora* not through the eyes of a young director trying to ship his game in a year but through the eyes of a series producer who'd been developing games for nearly two decades. And there was a lot that Aonuma wanted to fix the second time around. "I wrote in a bunch of comments on where I thought things weren't good. Like, *I'm sorry that this comes from the one that made it this way, but...*"

"That was on the top of every list," said Mikiharu Ōiwa, a member of the 3DS remake team.

"*At the time, I think there was something wrong with me…*" added Aonuma.

So while Aonuma was proud of *Majora*'s hard reputation, it's ultimately Aonuma's many proposed changes that speak the loudest. "What I'm really happy for now," he said, "was the opportunity to address some of the things that made the game difficult in the wrong ways."

Some changes simply allowed the game to catch up to modern expectations. The frame rate increased. The team also added a fully rotatable 3D camera for 3DS and 2DS models with a second stick.

There were also a lot of gameplay improvements. The Song of Double Time was made more useful. A new sidequest was added involving the Gorman brothers, and with it a seventh glass bottle to collect. All the bosses were reworked to be more fun and to better communicate their weaknesses. A Sheikah Hint Stone beside the Happy Mask Salesman was added to offer video clips as hints for what to do next.

In addition to the game's many tweaks, a fishing activity was added. Aonuma seemed particularly excited about this. "You can go fishing!" he told *Famitsu* before the remake was out. "I'm not sure if you'll have time to fish in the world of *Majora's Mask*… […] But we've added a fishing hole. Two of them, in fact."

"So with the moon slowly falling down on you, you go fishing?" asked the interviewer, laughing.

"That's right," Aonuma said. "I wanted to give the players a feeling like 'I know the world is about to end and I'm going fishing! I'm a badass!'" Aonuma playfully frames the addition of a frivolous minigame as an exercise in futility. Why would you fish if the world is about to end? But on the other hand, why *not* fish? Why do anything? Like the rest of the game, it's an existential puzzle without a clear answer.

Another refrain about the original *Majora* is that a lot of people who *did* play through and beat *Majora* never realized how many missions they had missed in Clock Town, accidentally skipping much of Koizumi and Takano's handiwork.

To that end, the team vastly improved the Bomber's Notebook, a day planner for tracking the whereabouts of each of the game's important characters throughout the three days. In the N64 original, the notebook is vague and sometimes unhelpful. The new notebook, easily accessed on the 3DS's second screen, tracks your quests for you and even offers an alarm to let you know when an event is happening relevant to the quest you're working on.

Aonuma much preferred these kinds of changes instead of making the game artificially easier by nerfing bosses and enemies. "I repetitively told the staff to never make this game easier. For example, when you fight the bosses, I believe that you gain true satisfaction after you try many different things, and finally take the right steps to defeat it." After all, deaths were never the kind of difficulty players of the original version complained about.

As Tomohiro Yamamura, another member of the 3DS team, put it, "We focused our energy on how well we can communicate the meanings of the missions to the players. By doing this, I think we were able to make the challenges more comprehensible while keeping the same level of challenge as the Nintendo 64 version."

They did a fantastic job—creating the overdue final draft of a game that was always begging for some quality-of-life improvements. If *Majora*'s greatest sin is how much it requires you to beat your head against the wall, then the 3DS remake offers a helmet.

But *even better* than added signposts, like the Hint Stone and improved Bomber's Notebook, would be a more thoroughly baked-in design that makes it more possible to figure out for yourself what to do next. Fans would have to wait until the release of *Breath of the Wild* to see a Zelda game nail this kind of subtle, almost subliminal environmental nudging. But these are design challenges that take more than a year to solve.

THE INNER CIRCLE

ONE OF MY FAVORITE WORKS of/about critical interpretation is *Room 237*, a feature-length video essay in which several people offer up their unified theories about the secret meaning of Stanley Kubrick's film adaptation of *The Shining*. Each narrator fluently defends his or her own pet theory—that the film is secretly about the Holocaust, or secretly about the slaughter of the Native Americans, or secretly about the American government's faking of the moon landing.

The film uses shots from *The Shining* to help make each theorist's point, but presents each without comment, ultimately siding with no one or everyone—so that not only is *Room 237* a great case for *The Shining* as an open text, but *Room 237* is *itself* an open text that sustains multiple interpretations.

I'll say for myself that, when I first watched *Room 237* in the theater, I thought the filmmaker was slyly making fun of the theorists—who do sometimes come across as crackpots. But when I streamed *Room 237* at home by myself and away from the cackles of the audience, it seemed to me that the filmmaker presented the theories much more earnestly, possibly even with admiration for the depth of their study… even though the theorists are likely reading things that weren't originally intended to be there.

The human mind constantly searches for patterns in everything—and often finds them. One of the theorists in the film tells the story of how he discovered that *The Shining* was about the Holocaust at just the time in his life when he was thinking about the Holocaust. He doesn't understand that when he was presented with a confounding film, his naturally interpretive mind reached for what he'd already been pondering.

Still, the specificity and personality of his interpretation is what's so cool about the movie and about art itself. The meaning found in the work is not decided by just the creator or just the players—it is instead a negotiation between both parties.

Fan theories are so creative, weird, charming, and even convincing—but what I love most is that even the best theories say more about us than they do about whatever we're discussing. We are often so deliberate and constructed in how we talk about ourselves, but when we put our attentions on another object, we let our guards down and candidly fill that object with our hopes, fears, loves, and insecurities.

The best fan theories tend to tap into feelings that are already in the source text. The "Five Stages" theory highlights the game's actual wide range of emotions. The "Link is Dead" theory highlights the game's actual exploration of death. The "Termina = Lorule = The Dark World" theory highlights just how interested the Zelda series is in exploring the world's duality, as good and bad places that exist on top of one another.

"The exhortation to just absorb mystery, not solve it, is one of those arguments that makes a certain amount of sense until you think about it," writes Jeff Jensen in his *Entertainment Weekly* interview with David Lynch. "How do I do that? Should I take that posture with any story? Are you actually encouraging me to be a couch potato? The argument that people should be passive consumers of storytelling designed to entertain by stimulating curiosity is a paradox I can't quite reconcile. Playing detective with mystery fiction is part of the enjoyment of the genre. Just as romance fans 'ship, mystery nerds theorize."

As Jensen points out, intellectual curiosity is only natural. But I think there's an even more fundamental reason why we theorize: It puts us into community with one another.

•

Since we've existed, humans have wanted each other's approval. One way to gain that approval is to know things that the others in your group do not. Another way is to pretend to.

"In almost every ancient religion," my dad told me, "there are the religious beliefs themselves that are available to the common man, the world at large. And then there's *the secret knowing*. The enlightenment that is available only to those who are able to tune into it, who have achieved a level of spirituality that is elitist… special… unique. Which is very attractive because you're not just out there doing this with the hoi polloi, you are among the inner circle."

"What do you think it says about us as people that we are so attracted to secret meaning?" I asked.

"At the most basic level," my dad said, "we all want to feel we're special. Nobody wants to be ordinary. If you can achieve or perceive or figure out something that sets you apart, you know you're not ordinary anymore. You're not part of the great unwashed, the man on the street, the woman on the street. You've joined an inner circle." This can go beyond feelings of superiority, though. "Sometimes, in our desperation to be included, we will give up our integrity, our pride—pretty much anything to be accepted. You're not always making choices based on higher values. You just want to do whatever it takes to be accepted and loved and part of the in-crowd."

In a Kotaku article about fan theories, Merritt K explains the far-fetched theory of the Donkey Kong universe's Great Ape War that the Donkey Kong Wikia tells us was fought "between the Kongs (aka the Primate Alliance) and the Kremlings (aka the Kroc-Army) thought to have taken place sometime between *Donkey Kong 3* and *Donkey Kong Country*." The wiki offers a detailed synopsis, which is impressive considering the grisly struggle is never referenced in any Donkey Kong games.

K presents fan theories like the Great Ape War as our makeshift replacement for the once-hot commodity of video game codes and secrets now that we live in an age where everything can be looked up online and false rumors can be rooted out with the quick hacking of a game's code.

According to K, the theories attempt to re-imbue solved games with mystery. "If you tell me that Luigi is in *Super Mario 64*, I can tell you that you are lying or misinformed," she writes. "The conversation is over. But if instead, you tell me that *Super Mario Bros. 3* is a stage performance within the Mario universe, I can offer no such rebuttal. I might argue against your claim, or I might consider its implications. But short of the rare Word of God, nobody can finally arbitrate this claim.[11] The conversation can continue forever. […] In a media

---

11 Here, "Word of God" refers to the creator (Miyamoto, in this example) offering a definitive answer. Which he eventually did: It's a play.

landscape dominated by crossover superhero movies and post-*Lost* TV shows that present themselves as puzzles, and in which the code of video games is no longer impenetrable and mysterious, it makes perfect sense that fans would dive into the stories of games."

This trend seems to go well beyond the realm of games. All of us gravitate toward groups, be it based on shared ideals, common interests, race, or religion. Having knowledge and skills that are useful to your group makes you more likely to survive and bear offspring. In some groups throughout history, your group needs you because you can fish. At some points in history, you can signal to you group, "You guys need me because I'm the only one here who can fish." At others, it may be most useful to signal, "You guys need me because I'm the only one who's noticing what *Westworld* is setting up for Season 3."

The most concise iteration of this point comes from the poet Elisa Gabbert in her book *The Self Unstable*: "All species evolve toward overspecialization. If you find anything other than food or sex interesting, it's signaling."

That drive to be a cool kid within one's social circle never leaves us, not even those among us who've managed to achieve it. Aonuma's star has risen since he made *Majora*. He's now been entrusted with the Zelda franchise for longer than anyone, longer even than Zelda's creator.

And yet even as he's received awards, fan worship, and rave reviews, Aonuma remains in Miyamoto's shadow.

Once, after the release of *The Wind Waker*, he even tried to quit over it. "I told Mr. Shigeru Miyamoto that I didn't want to be the director anymore," Aonuma said in the Fujisawa interview. He cited the "heavy workload" as one reason, but it sounded as if the main reason was his boss. "Mr. Miyamoto points out every mistake that I made in front of the reporters!"

Aonuma offered the example of reporters often asking, "What makes a game a Zelda game?" Aonuma noticed that Miyamoto answered the question differently at different times: "In one interview he answered, 'Zelda games are unique,' and then in another he suggested, 'Zelda games demonstrate growth.'" So then when it was his turn to answer, Aonuma would give one of Miyamoto's answers, "only to be interrupted by Mr. Miyamoto himself disagreeing with me saying, 'No, that's different,' in front of all the reporters!"

Miyamoto sometimes comes off as an asshole in the typical way that bosses are assholes—and other times an asshole in the typical way that rock stars are assholes. How could he not be a jerk sometimes, considering how long he's been on top? He's excitable, fun, creative, curious, and precise, but also distracted, withholding, and a little cruel—and carries with him the adoration of tens of millions wherever he goes. He's worked hard to keep the childlike spark alive inside himself—which is no small feat in your mid-60s—but sometimes employees simply need a boss to let them know when they're doing a good job. It seems to me that "creating and sustaining mystery" is much more admirable as an artistic goal than it is as a management style.

Aonuma is as aware of all this as anyone, but unlike most game developers, he stands a chance of being up on Video Game Mount Rushmore beside his mentor. Aonuma told Fujisawa in their conversation, "I think that Mr. Miyamoto is a great man, but someday I want to surpass him. [...] I heard there are people overseas who worship Mr. Miyamoto like God, but I'm not like that. And I think I'll exceed him some day."

But if I know Aonuma—if I know people—even if he gets there, it'll never be enough. The work could always be better. The artist could always be more admired. We want so badly to be in the inner circle. As Skull Kid discovers, sometimes you get the power you seek—but it never feels like you thought it would.

REALITY OVER REALISM

BEFORE I BOUGHT MY OWN copy of *Hyrule Historia*, I only knew about the book's most famous two pages that had been feverishly cited and screenshotted throughout the internet—the series timeline.

However, the book contains a note from Aonuma to fans that has been mentioned far less often. "'The History of Hyrule' allows players to determine where each Zelda game is positioned in the chronology of the series," begins Aonuma. "One thing to bear in mind, however, is that the question the developers of the Legend of Zelda series asked themselves before starting on a game was, 'What kind of game play should we focus on?' rather than 'What kind of story should we write?'

"Because the games were developed in such a manner," Aonuma continues, "it could be said that Zelda's story lines were afterthoughts." Including the fact that *Skyward Sword* kicks off the Zelda timeline. "Flipping through the pages of 'The History of Hyrule,' you may even find a few inconsistencies. However, peoples such as the Mogma tribe and items such as the Beetle that appear in *Skyward Sword* may show up again in other eras. Thus, it is my hope that the fans will be broad minded enough to take into consideration that this is simply how Zelda is made."

Look, says the creator, *this lore is not all gonna wrap up in a neat package. Because that's nowhere near our primary concern.*

If we want Aonuma's realest answer to the question of the Zelda timeline, we must look back to a 2002 IGN interview conducted long before he had a Zelda book to promote. When the interviewer asks how *The Wind Waker* squares with the series timeline, Aonuma replies, "In our opinions, with the Legend of Zelda, every game has a new Link. A new hero named Link always rises to fight evil." By this point, Aonuma had begun to sound less like a Story Guy and more like his mentor.

When Iwata asks Miyamoto about story in "Iwata Asks," Miyamoto replies, "The stories in The Legend of Zelda may not match up as the series progresses. We actually expend a lot of time trying to make them match up though. It would make things a lot easier if the players said, 'Oh, that doesn't really matter.'"

Iwata laughs and says, "You would rather spend your energy making game elements rather than the story."

"That's right," Miyamoto says. "Sometimes people ask whether Yoshi is a boy or a girl. If I answer, 'Probably a boy,' then they say, 'So a boy is laying eggs?' But the moment I say Yoshi lays eggs and so Yoshi must be a girl, they'll say, 'Then Yoshi's voice needs to sound more like a girl's!' But I want to make video games without having to worry about such background info."

Perhaps the act of interpreting games turns us into story people.

Perhaps the act of making games turns us into mechanics people.

•

An irony of producing art is that artists work so hard to deliberately construct something that they hope will not feel deliberately constructed.

And if a work has reached that point where it feels *fully itself*, that's also the point where we are paradoxically less inclined to give credit to the artist. What could *Abbey Road* ever be but itself? Despite documentary footage of petty in-fighting and early takes where Harrison sings extra lyrics over the instrumental break in "Something," *Abbey Road* was always going to be *Abbey Road*… right? The hard work of four musicians and a producer has now passed into the realm of inevitability.

I think that's why we should believe Aonuma and company when they say they are happy that people are reading so deeply into *Majora*. It feels great to see people engage with your work, to talk about your characters as if they are real. It's an honor to have your creation become the object of another person's obsession, even as that obsession takes them in directions you never would have expected.

That's also why creators are so often reticent to tell a fan that their experience with the work is *wrong*. The game is out—it's the player's experience now, not the creators'. After all, the experience of art doesn't exist until you read, view, or play it—and each of us reads, views, and plays through our own unique lens. This is never truer than in video games due to the additional layer of interactivity—my playthrough will necessarily look different from yours.

But even when you are reading a book, let's say *this* book, you are in charge of the experience in so many ways. Whether you read deeply or skim. Whether you dip into the book across several months or zip through it in one night. Whether you think the voice of the book seems friendly or boring or surly or profoundly erotic. Whether you mentally hear the words with an accent from California or Massachusetts or Virginia or Missouri—all places I've actually lived. Whether or not you've played *Majora* before reading. Whether or not you've read other titles in this book series that might change your expectations for what you'll encounter in this entry.

If you want to play *Majora* as Dead Link, no one can stop you. Or if you want to play with Kübler-Ross's

On Death and Dying open in front of you, no one can stop you. Or if you want to turn *Majora* into a simple adventure game and leave Clock Town every chance you get. Or if you want to 100% the game, including all the archery and 3DS fishing. Or if you want to learn to speedrun it, exploiting glitches to beat the world record time of 25 minutes and 15 seconds.

It's when you declare your own way of playing/seeing the game to be *canon* that you go from "human having an artistic experience" to "least pleasant commenter on the Let's Play video."

One of the coolest features of the indie RPG *Undertale* is the existence of the pacifist route, a way to get through the entire game without ever killing a single enemy. Or it was cool until fans of the game took to bullying anyone who dared stream *Undertale* while playing in any way other than the pacifist route. "It got kinda ridiculous for a while—people insisting that people playing the Genocide route were legitimately horrible people," an *Undertale* fan named BabyCharmander told Kotaku's Chloe Spencer for an article about the game's toxic fan culture. "I was seeing people being 100% serious when they compared people who played that route to child abusers and murderers."

That's where benign fandoms become toxic fandoms. If you have a deep allegiance to a very specific set of parameters for a "correct" Zelda game, you may be first in line to Twitter rant if Aonuma dares produce an "incorrect" Zelda game.

This is especially true when a love of lore tends to be offered as a justifiable reason for intolerance, like: Sorry, but gay characters have no place in Harry Potter. And: Sorry, but black people just aren't stormtroopers. And: Sorry, but there's no such thing as a female Ghostbuster.[12]

Holding on to anything too tightly threatens to destroy it. Playing notes too mechanically robs the musician of opportunities for intonation and interpretation. Wanting to do nothing but hang out at home with your significant other breeds codependence and incites entire wars over dishes. Needing an improv show to go perfectly gets you way too far in your own head to listen to your scene partners. And needing new entries in a video game series to adhere to strict rules makes games that are lifeless and dull.

•

12   Likewise, there can occasionally be a disquieting overlap between playful theorizing about the arts and destructive "theorizing" about the world. People who come to believe that climate change is fake, or that vaccinations are bad, or that the Sandy Hook Elementary shooting never happened may find stimulation and community in their false beliefs, but they're all doing real harm. Many truths are closed texts.

In his GDC talk, Aonuma explores a core design principle of Miyamoto's, which is that the Zelda series "values reality over realism."

Whereas realism attempts "to faithfully replicate the real world to whatever extent possible," Zelda is more about "making players feel like what they are experiencing is real." Aonuma presents the cel-shading in *The Wind Waker* as an example of how "exaggerated expression" can actually make the game experience "feel more real," offering the following example: One night, Link steps into a Bomb Shop, and the owner merely says, "Welcome," or, "This is a Bomb Shop." According to Aonuma, this purely informational line does not pass Miyamoto's reality test because it does not acknowledge anything about the setting, the time of night, or the characters themselves. His example of a better response?

> Are you alone, kid? Where are your parents?
> This is a BOMB Shop. This is no place for
> kids to come in the middle of the night. You
> be a good kid now and run on home… Well,
> that's what I should say, but the thing is these
> pirates came and stole my bombs, so business
> hasn't been good lately. I tell you what, I'll sell
> you bombs if you promise not to cause any
> trouble for my shop.

Aonuma notes that because players "tend to forget that Link is just a child," this kind of line allows the player to remember, "Oh! That's right! I'm just a boy," and draws the player deeper into the game world. In *Majora*, we see this kind of reality when characters treat you differently depending on what mask you're wearing—you're constantly reminded who you are and/or who you're pretending to be.

This, I believe, is often one of the differences between how creators approach their work and how many fans do. Creators attempt to expand a work by highlighting/exaggerating elements so those elements can "feel more real" than reality. Fans often fall into the trap of begging a work to remain tethered to reality (or *a* reality). Adhering to timeline continuity is the opposite of fostering a fertile space for creative expression.

People fell in love with *The Hobbit* and the Lord of the Rings books because they felt a deep connection to the big cast of well-drawn characters and the expansive, dangerous world, not because the lore proceeded as logically as possible. Tolkien himself disappeared up the ass of his own lore with historical Middle Earth snooze, *The Silmarillion*, doing away with pesky conventions like character, scene, prose style, and emotion so he could offer up pure unfettered history of a made-up world. It was only when his publisher rejected an early draft of this boring book that he began writing the beloved

Rings trilogy. My working definition of a "fans-only" book, movie, or game is a work that capitalizes on your emotional attachment to a franchise while doing nothing to actively further that attachment.

A lot of our great works do not concern themselves with continuity. Mario's adventures don't pretend to follow an overarching plot across the series—not even the games helmed by "story person" Koizumi. The Simpson family's ages remain in stasis even as time marches forward through the decades. And even though we fans borrow the word "canon" from Christianity, the Bible itself doesn't even pretend to have continuity: The Old Testament begins with two dissimilar creation stories, and the New Testament begins with three variations on the life of Jesus and then presents a fourth gospel that is wildly different in tone, message, and yes, timeline.

Freshness, then, comes not from a slavish devotion to Zelda lore but rather to a desire to mix things up with every game. "As creators, it wouldn't be any fun to simply continue making the same thing over and over again," says Aonuma in his GDC talk. "We have continued creating new Zelda titles over the last few years without changing our core team members. […] Being able to take the regrets of the last title and make them a theme for the next is extremely effective and leads us to decisions related to change and continuity."

Majora was a reaction to *Ocarina*. *The Wind Waker* was a reaction to *Majora*. *Twilight Princess* was a reaction to *The Wind Waker*. Your favorite Zelda was based on a risk taken to avoid merely replicating past successes. Even the first game in the series was created on the premise that it not be too much like *Super Mario Bros.*

•

Majora's Mask is a game in which you encounter people who are going through different phases of denial or acceptance of the end of the world, or they're mourning the loss of their lives. If you work to unite Anju and Kafei, it's a short reunion. "Please take refuge," Kafei tells you. "We are fine here. We shall greet the morning… together." And so the couple huddles together in the Stock Pot Inn, glad to be reunited but still doomed.

That's just one of the many times *Majora* delves into the dark implications of mortality in a way that is rare for a Nintendo game. I believe that what the game would ask of us is to simply sit with those emotions. Feel the feelings! Empathize with the characters. But a lot of those feelings are kind of uncomfortable to sit in.

"Real art has the capacity to make us nervous," writes Susan Sontag in "Against Interpretation." "By reducing the work of art to its content and then interpreting that, one tames the work of art. Interpretation makes art manageable, conformable."

I was chewing on this aloud to my dad, the preacher, and we got to talking about the gospel of John. John is the one of the four canonized gospels of Jesus, written decades later than the other three, and it's way different than the others—in part because it was written with the gnostic crowd in mind, a group who, as my dad explained, was very much into the idea that "spiritual enlightenment was available only to the chosen few."

"If you read the Gospel of John," my dad said, "what John almost always says is, 'True knowledge is love.' So it's a slam—or if not that, at least an answer—to the Gnostic heretics, as they came to be called. Whether it's a Pharisee, a Sadducee, or even an Essene, they all had their own secret stuff. And John is saying, 'You're missing it. The true knowledge is available to anyone.'"

"And isn't that slam couched in the promise that truth is simpler than you're acting like it is?" I asked.

"Yeah!" my dad said. "It's simpler to understand but it's harder to live."

"It's sort of easy," I said, "to enjoy a convoluted theory that doesn't ask anything of you."

"Yeah," my dad said, "try *loving your enemies*."

If you can condition yourself to get used to all that is messy and loose and playful and even incoherent about art, you are also conditioning yourself to handle all that is messy and loose and complex and challenging about this life you are living. The human mind can concoct ways to make things appear tidy. It's good that it can. It's necessary. But at the subatomic level when you zoom way in? And at the cosmic level when you zoom way out? It's all chaos.

SAVING THE WORLD

THE ZELDA FAN CLUB GREW a lot bigger in 2017 following the release of *Breath of the Wild* for Switch and Wii U. Link's finest, funnest adventure has outsold everything else in the series—even *Ocarina*. The press crowned it 2017's Game of the Year because it *was* the game of the year. There's more fun to be had, more room for my own creativity, more secrets to uncover, more atmospheric storytelling, more brain puzzles, and more satisfying combat than in any previous Zelda game.

To my mind, *Breath* so successfully iterates on nearly everything that made *Ocarina* good *and* adds so much more that it effectively renders *Ocarina* obsolete. You like horses? *Breath* has a sophisticated, top-notch horse-taming and bonding system. You like puzzles? There's a new puzzle every twenty feet. You want a good hero's journey? *Breath* opens on a cryogenic(ish)ly frozen hero from a bygone era who must leave the safety of his cave and venture out to tame a vast, deadly world on the brink of obliteration, overcoming his lost memory and past failures to become the Joseph Campbell-approved hero of Hyrule. You like hang gliders? My friend… maybe you should sit down because I have good news.

The one place that *Breath* doesn't stick the landing is plot and character. The characters you meet are often both broad and nonspecific, rarely leaving a strong impression. Many women you encounter have oddly childish and/or sexualized voices. The English-language Zelda chews the scenery on every line reading. The Ganon bosses look like the sort of bland, swirly horror the Avengers would fight two hours into a movie that was fun for a while but is now starting to lose me. The plotline in which an amnesiac Link goes searching for memories fails because the memories are boring cutscenes from a war whose outcome is all around us. The game's best characters are the common enemies of Hyrule: The Bokoblin, Lizalfos, and Moblins are well-scripted, reactive, and totally at home in their environments—the perfect combination of dangerous and funny. Tellingly, none of them ever says a word.

If you were new to the franchise, I'd tell you to start with *Breath*, then pick up a Switch or an SNES Mini and play *A Link to the Past*, which is the Zelda game that has the most (to borrow a term from Yacht Club) "gameplay per square inch." And once you've spent a couple of games in Hyrule, you'd be ready to depart for *Majora*. *Ocarina* is off the shortlist. Not because it isn't great, but because nearly every way that it's great has been improved upon—whereas nearly every way *Majora* is great continues to stand out all these years later.

Aonuma, for his part, has been surprised that more games have not tried to ape *Majora*'s odd magic. "When I finished creating *Majora's Mask*," he told Iwata, "I assumed that other companies would be releasing games similar to this one. But in reality, no one did. Even fifteen years after the Nintendo 64 version of this game released, no one created a game like this. Because of this, the unique taste and feel of this game seems to exist for a long time…"

Iwata asked if Aonuma would call the unique taste "timeless," and Aonuma agreed that he would. "So even if people of [the younger] generation play this game, I think they can find something that will call out to their hearts."

Even if game studios did make games inspired by *Majora*, a game like *Majora* has nothing to fear when a game like *Breath* comes out because *Majora's* charms are not technological and cannot be iterated upon. It's too singular, too weird, too dark, too risky. Its villains are a malevolent mask, a sad little boy, and a rictus-grinning moon.

But weird isn't all of it. The other reason *Majora* endures has to do with how the game defines heroism.

•

"As much as [*Majora*] is about exploring dungeons," writes Jason Leung in his Nintendo.com diary, "*Majora's Mask* is about helping people. You spend a lot of time changing the courses of many lives, like a man who was wronged by a thief, a ranch girl whose cows are terrorized by aliens, and a Goron baby who won't stop crying."

When I interviewed him over coffee, it's this theme that Leung was most eager to talk about all these years later. We were nearly two hours into our conversation when I asked him if there was anything else he took from his experience of working on the game—an open-ended question that could well have been restated as, "What else do you remember?"

Leung replied, "[*Majora's*] story. There aren't extras. Everybody has their own story. And I think that really helped inform how I aspire to write things—everybody has a backstory. There are no incidental characters or events or accidents. Everything has its effects."

"I've heard that about good screenwriting too," I offered. "Everybody feels like the protagonist of their own story."

"Exactly," said Leung. "In their own world, they're the star. Before *Majora*, all the NPCs were just kind of there to deliver you something or to help move what you're doing farther along. But here there were real consequences. They had an impact on another character and another character. You could see the changes."

It's telling that when Aonuma had the option to add whatever he wanted to the 3DS remake of *Majora*, he added a fishing game. Fishing is quiet, meditative, and more than a little bit mundane—but it's one of many tiny human moments that *Majora* exists to honor. Daily life, normally so hard to savor, is suddenly imbued with renewed gravity as the moon in the sky draws closer.

Unlike in most adventure games, these little moments are not window dressing, they are the point. Boys play hide-and-seek. Jugglers juggle. A shop owner sells wares. Builders worry over whether their project will get done on time. If I were to describe Clock Town's missions to you and you weren't familiar with the game, they would sound like disposable side quests. And if this were most games, you'd be right. To paraphrase a comment I once read on an article about *Majora*: *It's best to think of the game's world as one big dungeon. Everything is important.*

It's this aspect that Jonathan Holmes singles out in a thoughtful Destructoid article about *Majora*. "Link is the one who gets that we're about to die, and is willing to try to make a difference," Holmes writes. "He can't sit back and wait for others to take care of him. He has to take care of himself, and in doing so, everyone else. It's a challenge that's simultaneously scary, strange, beautiful, and anything but simple. Ask any interesting adult about their lives, and they'll likely use the same words to describe it."

To Holmes, Link's maturity comes from the fact that he has already saved the world once before in the events of *Ocarina*, and even did so in the body of a teenager—though no one in Termina knows it:

> *Majora's Mask* expects you to be able to access a higher level of motivation. Though the lingering fear of death is always there pushing you forward, the moment-to-moment decisions you make in the game are often driven by a combination of curiosity and optimism, with no guaranteed reward beyond experience. The game doesn't tell you you have to form an all fish-person rock band, or lead a parade of dogs through the town, but what if you did anyway? […] What if you did things to help people, just for the sake of helping, with death hanging over your head and no idea how to stop it?

The success of this theme helps explain my own distaste for the "Link is Dead" theory, which if true would render all this community irrelevant. *All the good people you helped? The farm girl, the young couple, the mummified dad? They were never real. They only existed for your edification.* The theory flattens *Majora* into the usual video game narcissist power fantasy, a play in which behind all this community service hides secret solipsism.

Majora is instead the rare hero's quest story that ultimately puts the community over the hero. While on one hand we get to feed our Western individualist egos—exploring dungeons, destroying villains, collecting magical antiquities—we also do errands for people so that their lives can improve a little just before we all die together. In that sense it is more truly Eastern than any other Zelda game. As Holmes puts it, the game "expects you to have the empathy, tolerance for hardship, and the willingness to live in the moment *for the sake of the moment*."

There's little glory in the final showdown, which denies you your faceoff with Skull Kid and sends you instead onto the moon—a serene place covered in grass where the doomsday clock for once has stopped. Five children hang out beneath a large tree, four of whom offer optional challenges while the fifth wears Majora's Mask. When that kid asks, "Will you play… with me?" it's your yes that begins the game's final battle. A scary and challenging three-stage fight follows in which Majora spins and flies and whips you with tentacles, but all in the context of two kids playing a game. Play or don't—but you won't be urged on by a final rousing speech.

Nor will you be celebrated with a ticker tape parade if you win. Even when you win, your only reward is to keep going. Termina isn't an end: It was just one stop on a quest that spans multiple adventures and multiple dimensions across multiple timelines by multiple Links. And although he makes it back to Hyrule, there is no evidence that the Link of *Ocarina* and *Majora* will ever find Navi, the lost fairy friend whose search incited his entire adventure in Termina. With Link's luck, it seems more likely that he'll happen upon some new threat—demonic cackling overheard in Gerudo Valley, say, or finding the people of Kakariko Village under the influence of a "new" sorcerer known only as "Nonag." The grind will continue.

Carolyn Petit points out in an article for Vice that Link saves the world and then doesn't even make it to the afterparty. "Well… it's almost time for the carnival to begin…" says his ice-cold fairy companion, Tael. "So why don't you just leave and go about your business? The rest of us have a carnival to go to." Lest we think for a moment that our good deed was not its own reward, Link obeys. As Petit concludes, "The hero's path is often a lonely one."

Often, 2020 feels to me like an alienating time to be alive. Mass shootings end lives and fracture communities daily. Billionaires consolidate wealth and power at our expense. COVID-19 has put a moratorium on hangouts, hookups, and hugs. The president sows hate, fear, and violence, imprisons children in cages, and works to hasten the actual impending ecological apocalypse. Each of us has to decide what kind of hero we want to be: Will we go off adventuring to save the world through direct action? Will we take care of our friends, family, and neighbors in the face of so much pain? Is there time in the next 72 hours to somehow do both?

I'm reminded of something Romani's older sister Cremia says earlier in the game. After you fight off the masked Gorman brothers and help her complete her milk run to Clock Town, she gives you Romani's Mask (the cow mask), which allows you entrance to the adults-only Milk Bar. And then she says, "With every good deed, a child takes one step closer to adulthood." And while it's a weird justification for giving a nine-year-old the Termina equivalent of a fake ID, it's also a beautiful distillation of *Majora*'s greatest theme.

Online I've seen *Majora* called "hipster Zelda," and it's true that *Majora* is the Zelda game the cool kids seem to go for. It's different. Darker. A deeper cut. But in another way, it's the least hipster Zelda. Cool is called "cool" because it means *emotionally* cool—closed off, disaffected, possibly vaping, hiding eyes behind shades. *Majora* isn't disaffected at all. It's a game about love, fear, mourning, and sacrifice. Its protagonist is a little elf boy who just can't stop helping people. Link feels everything!

In the game's final scene, back in the woods of Hyrule, Link and Epona ride off together into the sun. And then we see what Skull Kid has carved into a tree stump: an etching of Link and Skull Kid, hand in hand, the four giants in the background, the fairies Tatl and Tael hovering above: a community of old and new friends who have seen Skull Kid at his worst and accept him anyway.

If the hallmark of hipsterdom is ironic distance, I don't see a bit of hipster in *Majora's Mask* or its earnest adoring fans. All *Majora* fans, even the ones who've concocted theories that I do not agree with, are responding to the same great things in the game I am. We'll corner each other at a party and yes, we will argue about this game that we love, but we might be friends by the end of the night. And isn't connecting with others the whole point of both *Majora* and fan culture itself?

Majora's Mask is about loving the people you meet on your journey. It's about helping people when you can and making peace with not being able to please everyone at once. It's about forgiving good people who did bad things. It's about making good use of the little time you've got. These are simple, "E for Everyone" themes available to anyone. The truth is sitting right there on the surface, and sometimes the surface is enough.

NOTES

A Cursed Cartridge

The text of "Ben Drowned" has been collected in several places, including the Creepypasta Wiki: https://bit.ly/3eQY5bJ.

Victor Luckerson's article "The Cult of 'Zelda: Majora's Mask': How the internet warped a video game into real-life horror" was published at The Ringer on March 3, 2017: https://bit.ly/36XUrdr.

The Story Guys

Game Informer's Ben Hanson sat down with Shigeru Miyamoto and Eiji Aonuma in early 2017 for a video interview. The video, "The Storytelling of the Legend of Zelda," features Miyamoto's "meat and substance" quote, and was published February 15, 2017: https://bit.ly/2zZBDOT.

Chris Kohler's book *Power-Up: How Japanese Video Games Gave the World an Extra Life*, originally published in 2005 by BradyGames, recounts Aonuma's interview experience at Nintendo.

The 1UP Interview with Aonuma, "Linked-In: Meet the Man Behind Zelda" conducted by Thomas Puha and Sam Kennedy, was posted to 1UP on October 16, 2007 and is currently available at the Internet Archive: https://bit.ly/3cvgl95.

Miyamoto's interview with the New York Times was Simon Parkin's December 29, 2017 piece "Nintendo's Switch Brings Some Magic Back": https://nyti.ms/2pUK4oS.

The 2017 conversation between Jin Fujisawa (Dragon Quest series) and Aonuma was posted on the Japanese site Denfami Nico Gamer on June 9, 2017 6/9/17 in both Japanese and English. The English version, titled "Talk: Latest Zelda's making process & 'Ocarina of Time' proposal disclosed [Nintendo Eiji Aonuma x SQEX Jin Fujisawa]," can be found here: https://bit.ly/36VEGDQ.

Aonuma's 2004 GDC talk was translated by Nintendo's Bill Trinen, transcribed by IGN, and originally posted as text to IGN on March 25, 2004 as "GDC 2004: The History of Zelda: Eiji Aonuma speaks about the essence of Zelda". https://bit.ly/2XYCDuH.

Jason Cipriano's interview with Aonuma was posted to Spike TV's website on October 17, 2013 as "A Look at 'The Legend of Zelda: A Link Between Worlds' with Series Producer Eiji Aonuma." It can be currently found archived at the Internet Archive: https://bit.ly/36XVcmN.

Chris Kohler interviewed Yoshiaki Koizumi in the December 4, 2007 Wired feature "Interview: Super Mario Galaxy Director on Sneaking Stories Past Miyamoto": https://bit.ly/2zWv4g0.

The 2017 Reddit AMA with Koizumi was conducted on June 14, 2017 as "Hi, I'm Mr. Koizumi, Producer of Super Mario Odyssey. AMA!": https://bit.ly/305AP5Z/.

Down the Rabbit Hole

Scott McCloud's *Understanding Comics* was first published in 1993.

The 2015 *Game Informer* print interview with Aonuma is partially excerpted online on Feb 21, 2015 by gameinformer. com as Kyle Hilliard's "Zelda Producer Eiji Aonuma Talks Creating Majora's Mask And His Personal Hobbies" (https://bit.ly/2BpehTe). Another part of the same interview is informally excerpted at Zelda Informer as "Eiji Aonuma Comments on the 5 Stages of Grief Theory, Wanted to Hook Players into the Emotional Tone" (https://bit.ly/303G8Td).

David Lynch's March 6, 1997 interview with *Rolling Stone*'s Mikal Gilmore is "David Lynch and Trent Reznor: The Lost Boys": https://bit.ly/378UpzP.

Building a 3D Zelda

The book quotes from several different entries in the "Iwata Asks" series:

- "The Legend of Zelda: Ocarina of Time 3D - Original Development Staff - Part 1" was published upon the release of the *Ocarina* 3DS remake. Iwata interviews Aonuma and Koizumi alongside Toshio Iwawaki, Takumi Kawagoe, and Toru Osawa, all of whom worked on the original *Ocarina*: https://bit.ly/2MrT7WR

- "The Legend of Zelda: Ocarina of Time 3D - Original Development Staff - Part 2" was also published upon the release of the *Ocarina* 3DS remake. Aonuma sticks around and is joined by Kazuaki Morita, Makoto Miyanaga, Satoru Takizawa, and Yoshiki Haruhana: https://bit.ly/2XrZjEy

- "The Legend of Zelda: Ocarina of Time 3D - Mr. Shigeru Miyamoto" was also published upon the release of the *Ocarina* 3DS remake. Iwata interviews Miyamoto solo: https://bit.ly/3gXaZan

- "Iwata Asks: The Legend of Zelda: Majora's Mask 3D" was published upon the release of the *Majora* 3DS remake. Iwata interviews Aonuma alongside remake team members Tomomi Sano, Tomohiro Yamamura, and Mikiharu Ooiwa: https://bit.ly/2MqB7Mv

IGN's rave 10/10 review of *Ocarina of Time* was Peer Schneider's "The Legend of Zelda: Ocarina of Time Review: The biggest game of the decade," first published November 25, 1998: https://bit.ly/2Xteg9l.

Playing Detective

D.F. Lovett defined fan theories in "What We Talk About When We Talk About Fan Theories," a November 21, 2016 post to his blog What Would Bale Do: https://bit.ly/2A1On7E.

The examples of movie fan theories cited in this chapter come from George Wales's article "25 mind-blowing movie fan theories to make you do a quadruple-take," posted June 22, 2017 to GamesRadar+: https://bit.ly/3eHCB0U.

Majora Fan Theories:

- The *Majora* fan theory that "it was all a dream" is raised by Kyle Hilliard in his 2015 *Game Informer* interview with Aonuma.

- The theories that Link and Tingle are the same person in different timelines and that there is a black hole that connects Termina to both Star Fox and F-Zero, are suggested in OrangeOctangular's May 24, 2014 Reddit post: https://bit.ly/2XvHBjA.

- The theory that *Majora*'s Stone Tower represents the Tower of Babel is suggested by Hylian Dan in his "The Message of Majora's Mask," posted to Zelda Universe on September 13, 2011: https://bit.ly/36W9MeN.

- The theory that Skull Kid is Link was posted to Reddit on July 31, 2012 by iatedeadpeople: https://bit.ly/2MrzL4e.

- The theory that *Majora* takes place in the middle of *Ocarina* comes from mybusterswords's September 27, 2016 Reddit post: https://bit.ly/3duXQTL.

- The theory that Termina was created by Majora so that Majora could possess Link's body is binbomsj's June 24, 2013 Reddit post: https://bit.ly/2XVh7qR.

- The theory that the events of *Majora* are actually just a play comes from jamesfulwiler's June 6, 2013 Reddit post: https://bit.ly/3gSaSg8

- The theory that Termina, Lorule, and the Dark World are all the same place comes from Lockstin & Gnoggin's YouTube video "Deepest Zelda Theory? The Cult of Masks": https://bit.ly/2zYeUD0.

- The theory that the four regions in Termina correspond to the four Greek types of love (*philia*, *eros*, *agape* and *storge*) comes from TheMaverickk's September 15, 2015 comment on Alasyn Eletha's "Zelda Theory: Five Stages of Grief," posted to Zelda Dungeon on September 12, 2015: https://bit.ly/2U8Uga5.

- The theory that the people of Ikana from *Majora* are actually the Dark Interlopers from *Twilight Princess* (a Zelda game that came out six years after *Majora*) comes from Eden Roquelaire's "Legend of Zelda Theory: Identity of the Dark Interlopers," posted on July 23, 2018 to Vocal: https://bit.ly/304wnEv.

- The theory that Majora's Mask itself contains the spirit of Ghirahim from *Skyward Sword* is from Razanak's May 12, 2016 YouTube video "Majora's True Identity? - Zelda Theory": https://youtu.be/rE5_EACskE0.

- The theory that the Happy Mask Salesman is the Hero of Termina in the same way that Link is the Hero of Hyrule comes from procrastoholic's June 30, 2013 Reddit post: https://bit.ly/2U772WO.

- The theory that Happy Mask Salesman is actually the true villain of *Majora's Mask* (and of *Ocarina of Time*) comes from "Ocarina of Time: The True Villain," posted to Some Ordinary Gamers Wiki on August 2, 2013: https://bit.ly/2MpZGcx.

- The theory that the Fierce Deity, and not Majora, is the game's true villain comes from Dr. Wily's April 15, 2015 YouTube video "Zelda Theory - MAJORA is the HERO?! (zelda majora's mask)": https://youtu.be/EofGUpWLVrs.

- The theory that Link and the citizens of Termina are cursed to continue reliving the same three days even after winning comes from Nexpo's October 13, 2018 YouTube video "Majora's Mask and the Art of Dark Symbolism": https://youtu.be/1kEFiocPLkI.

The Five Stages of Grief were first articulated by Elisabeth Kübler-Ross's 1969 book, *On Death and Dying*.

A definitive source for the theory that *Majora's Mask* reenacts Kübler-Ross's Five Stages of Grief is elusive, but the earliest citable mention is Brian Keen's September 2, 2010 post at Examiner titled "Majora's Mask: 5 of the 'zones' represent the 5 stages of grief," which can be found saved at the Internet Archive: https://bit.ly/36YKa0T.

Alex Plant's "Themes In Motion: Majora's Mask and the Five Stages of Grief," which cites Keen's piece, was posted to Zelda Dungeon on October 27, 2011, though attributed to Dathen Boccabella: https://bit.ly/3gPZ5ia. A January 19, 2020 comment on that post by user "Dathen" (presumably Boccabella) attempts to clear up the apparent misattribution.

The Zelda Dungeon article is cited by Matt Machmuller and Matthew Moffitt's September 16, 2013 Cracked article "6 Insane Video Game Fan Theories (That Make Total Sense)": https://bit.ly/2XVggXe.

The Game Theorists' video "Game Theory: Is Link Dead in Majora's Mask?" was posted to YouTube on November 9, 2013 (https://youtu.be/7S1SVkysIRw).

J Nicole Miller's "Which Video Games will my Future Children Play?" (https://bit.ly/36YfAUV), which references the Five Stages theory, was posted to GameSkinny on December 5, 2013.

Tristan Cooper's "5 Legend of Zelda Fan Theories That Make the Games Even Better" was posted on February 13, 2015 to Dorkly, now saved at the Internet Archive: https://bit.ly/305bQzG.

365 Days to Save Termina

The Hobonichi interview with Shigeru Miyamoto, Yoshiaki Koizumi, and Eiji Aonuma was published May 7, 2000 and can be found here at Hobonichi's website in six parts: https://bit.ly/2U8aReb. Part 1 of the six-part interview was translated into English by Canadian translator GlitterBerri and published to her blog: All quotes from Part 1 are from her November 20, 2012 translation, "Zelda Is Always Bringing Something New to the Table": https://bit.ly/2zYdyYT. Other quotes from Parts 2-6, previously untranslated into English, were translated by our own Michael P. Williams for inclusion in this book.

The 2015 *Famitsu* interview with Aonuma was translated as "Majora's Mask - The Reasons for the Creation and Rebirth" by user Kewl0210 and posted to the forum VGFacts on June 30, 2015: https://bit.ly/3eEQX2i.

The origin of "upending the tea-table" (Japanese, *chabu-dai-gaeshi*) as a concept has been traced to a scene in the Japanese baseball manga *Star of the Giants* (in Japanese, *Kyojin no Hoshi*), in which the angry father knocks over a table as he attacks his son. Images from the manga and the anime adaptation are provided by user Goritsu at Maniadō forums: https://bit.ly/2XsYueI.

Aonuma's views on Miyamoto were extracted from *GamesTM* by Nintendo Everything in a November 13, 2013 post titled "Aonuma talks about his views on Miyamoto, wants him to continue sharing opinions": https://bit.ly/2A1PxA2.

Something Interesting, Something New

Koizumi's quote about "what would happen if the moon started to fall towards Earth" comes from the August 2011 issue of *Official Nintendo Magazine*. The quote was excerpted by Thomas East's article "Zelda: Majora's Mask came to me in a dream - Koizumi" published July 5, 2011: https://bit.ly/3eGzI0q.

Toshiyuki Shikata was quoted in Sheryl Wudunn's September 1, 1998 article for the *New York Times* "North Korea Fires Missile Over Japanese Territory": https://nyti.ms/303IQrR.

The 2015 *Nintendo Dream* interview with Aonuma was published in issue 252, April 2015 (https://bit.ly/2MrB-bvA) and then partially translated and posted to Nintendo Everything on March 15, 2015 as "Aonuma talks about the creation of Zelda: Majora's Mask": https://bit.ly/2Xx6886.

The 2015 Kotaku interview with Aonuma was conducted by Stephen Totilo and published on February 17, 2015 as "How a Zelda Dungeon Is Made": https://bit.ly/2U7M89K/

The Nintendo Online Magazine interview with Miyamoto, Aonuma, and Mitsuhiro Takano was translated by N-Sider staff member Anthony JC (aka Anthony Calderon) and posted to N-Sider on April 16, 2004 as "The Making of the Game: Legend of Zelda - Majora's Mask": https://bit.ly/2XZ6eEs.

Majora is discussed on episode 222 of the podcast *Cane and Rinse*, "The Legend of Zelda: Majora's Mask," posted May 22, 2016: https://bit.ly/2U8hvkG

The Art of the Remix

The GameSpot interview where Koji Kondo described *Majora*'s score is Justin Haywald's "Creating Nintendo's Most Memorable Melodies: Q&A With Koji Kondo: Majora's Mask Memories and More," posted on December 14, 2014: https://bit.ly/2Xx6ED4.

8-bit Music Theory's video essay "The Music of Zelda's Overworld: a Historical Retrospective and Analysis" was posted to YouTube on October 22, 2016": https://youtu.be/BNH2pKfvyPQ.

Jake Butineau's video essay "Why Majora's Mask's Songs Are So Great (Game Music Discussion)" was posted to YouTube on August 17, 2017: https://youtu.be/5TmvMGy1D-0.

Laura Intravia and Brendon Shapiro's album *Shall We Play? Majora's Mask Piano Album* was officially released on August 4, 2016 by Video Games Live.

The French-language interview between Miyamoto and GameKult's William Audureau was posted November 1, 2012 as "Miyamoto, la Wii U et le secret de la Triforce": https://bit.ly/2z4IKFw.

Jason Leung's original Nintendo diary from June 5 through July 14, 2000, formerly available at Nintendo.com, can now be accessed through the Internet Archive as "Jason Leung (Author of English Screen Text) Diary Part I" and "Jason Leung Diary Part II": https://bit.ly/2XUVaIk.

Majora the Open Text

Patrick Klepek's "*Majora's Mask* Is a Game About Death" was posted to Kotaku on March 12, 2015: https://bit.ly/2BwyFC7.

Ruth Davis Konigsberg of *Time* magazine reported on the nuances of the Five Stages of Grief, and Kübler-Ross's own misgivings about the theory, in her January 29, 2011 article "New Ways to Think About Grief" (https://bit.ly/2AG-hopp). The 2007 research she cited was Paul K. Maciejewski, Baohui Zhang, Susan D. Block, and Holly G. Prigerson's "An Empirical Examination of the Stage Theory of Grief" published in volume 297, number 7 of the *Journal of the American Medical Association* (February 21, 2007): https://bit.ly/3gUCod0.

VortexxyGaming's "The Legend of Zelda Theory: The Five Stages of Grief" was posted to YouTube on September 3, 2015: https://youtu.be/nRaMR_SwmMo.

The portion of that early 2015 *Game Informe*r interview with Aonuma where he comments on the Five Stages of Grief interpretation was excerpted at Nintendo Everything as "Aonuma on the 5 stages of grief fan theory in Zelda: Majora's Mask" on March 4, 2015: https://bit.ly/306jidG/.

The section on how literary theorists would interpret Zelda is indebted to Purdue OWL's series of articles, "Literary Theory and Schools of Criticism": https://bit.ly/2Mqjg8H.

Entertainment Weekly's Jeff Jensen interviewed David Lynch in the May 1, 2017 feature "David Lynch thinks your Twin Peaks theories are 'a beautiful thing': Good, because we've got some": https://bit.ly/2XvOzoY.

The Flannery O'Connor quote comes from her essay "The Nature and Aim of Fiction," contained in her posthumous collection *Mystery and Manners: Occasional Prose* published by Farrar, Straus & Giroux in 1969.

Susan Sontag's essay "Against Interpretation" was collected in the 1966 book *Against Interpretation*, published by Farrar, Straus & Giroux.

American Songwriter interviewed Paul Simon in the October 7, 2011 feature "Interview: Paul Simon Discusses *Songwriter* and Songwriting": https://bit.ly/3cyux14.

David McRaney, author of the 2011 book *You Are Not So Smart* and a blog of the same name, wrote about pattern recognition in the September 11, 2010 post "The Texas Sharpshooter Fallacy": https://bit.ly/2zReO02.

Cultural Distance

Bill Trinen's 2003 Interview with *Game Informer* was posted to the web on October 10, 2003 as "Interview: Bill Trinen of Nintendo": https://bit.ly/2YcaIb1.

The 2015 GameSpot interview with Aonuma was conducted by Justin Haywald and posted on February 13, 2015 with the title "How Did Aliens Get Into The Legend of Zelda: Majora's Mask?: Dawn of the Final Day": https://bit.ly/2AyRaVW.

Sterling Anderson Osborne's master's thesis, *Linking Masks with Majora: The Legend of Zelda: Majora's Mask and Noh Theater*, was submitted to Florida Atlantic University in December 2014: https://bit.ly/2XtCIr8.

The Legend of Zelda and Theology was edited by Jonathan L. Walls and published by Gray Matter Books in 2011.

Majora's Evolving Legacy

The eerie television ad for *Majora* where "the world is waiting on you" has been uploaded to YouTube by Zelda Dungeon as "Majora's Mask Commercial #1 (Long)": https://youtu.be/Niwnnri4kyU.

The websites from the *Majora* web campaign are no longer active, but snapshots exist online of each at the Internet Archive:

- Radio Zelda: https://bit.ly/2U9m9yL

- Z-Science: https://bit.ly/3cxzA1T

- Survive with Binky! (binkypinkerson.com): https://bit.ly/3cxh6hS

- The End Times: https://bit.ly/2XtElVM

- Hogarth's Homepage of Hidden History (cryptochronology.org): https://bit.ly/3gRocRS

The Toys "R" Us *Majora* infomercial was uploaded to the Internet Archive by Retro Reality on April 27, 2011: https://bit.ly/2MpMswe.

Video Business magazine reported on Nintendo of America's $12 million marketing campaign for *Majora* in their November 6, 2000 issue (volume 20, number 45).

Reviews of *Majora's Mask*:

- IGN's 9.9/10 review of *Majora's Mask* was Fran Mirabella III's "Legend of Zelda: Majora's Mask: The Legend of Zelda continues. Could it be as glorious and perfect as The Ocarina of Time? Find out" first published October 25, 2000: https://bit.ly/2Xteg9l.

- Darren Zenko's review of *Majora's Mask*, "Majora's Mask a feast for the senses, an all-time high for Nintendo," was published in the *Edmonton Journal* on November 3, 2000.

- Peter Olafson and Charles Herold reviewed *Majora*—along with a slew of other video game titles—in the *New York Times* on November 16, 2000 as "Game Theory: New Video Game Reviews": https://nyti.ms/3cp2K3e.

- *The Guardian*'s Greg Howson reviewed *Majora* in the paper's November 22, 2000 "Games reviews" column: https://bit.ly/2UnFixh.

- GameSpot's 8.3/10 review of *Majora* was Jeff Gerstmann's "Majora's Mask is a great game, but it isn't for everybody": https://bit.ly/3dxnB5A

Sales figures and ranking for *Majora's Mask* are often circulated. VGChartz maintains data on sales for N64 games here: https://bit.ly/2Z9KBSe.

Aonuma praised *Majora*'s difficulty during the February 7, 2015 performance of "The Legend of Zelda: Symphony of the Goddesses's Master Quest" tour held at Tokyo International Forum. Footage of the show and of the interview was uploaded to Nintendo's YouTube channel on February 19, 2015: https://youtu.be/rlx29hKQSkc.

Siliconera reported on Aonuma's interview with *Famitsu* regarding *Majora 3D*'s new features on November 14, 2014 in "The Legend of Zelda: Majora's Mask 3D Changes Up Boss Fights, Adds Fishing": https://bit.ly/3dHxRbu.

The Inner Circle

The documentary film *Room 237* was directed by Rodney Ascher and released in 2012.

Merritt K's "The *Donkey Kong* Timeline Is Truly Disturbing" was published at Kotaku on November 21, 2019: https://bit.ly/3eQodDV.

Elisa Gabbert's *The Self Unstable* was published in 2013 by Black Ocean.

Reality Over Realism

Hyrule Historia was originally released in Japanese in 2011 by Shogakukan. Its English translation was released in 2013 by Dark Horse.

The 2002 IGN Interview with Miyamoto and Aonuma about *Wind Waker* was "Miyamoto and Aonuma on Zelda: The two masterminds divulge all about the latest Zelda," published on December 4, 2002: https://bit.ly/2U5zsAr.

Chloe Spencer reports on the toxic side of *Undertale*'s fandom in the Kotaku feature "The *Undertale* Drama": https://bit.ly/2XWTVs9.

Saving the World

Jonathan Holmes's Destructoid article "Majora's Mask is my favorite game about being a young adult" was published on November 9, 2014: https://bit.ly/2MsZ7i0.

Carolyn Petit's "In the Mouth of the Moon: A Personal Reading of 'Majora's Mask'" was published on March 3, 2015 at Vice: https://bit.ly/2Mqkqkn.

ACKNOWLEDGEMENTS

THANKS FOREMOST TO Boss Fight editor Michael P. Williams who gave feedback on multiple drafts, and also helped with research, translation, and putting the Notes section together. And to Boss Fight editor Alyse Knorr, whose notes helped nudge the book's thesis in a more rewarding and generous direction. Thanks also to the following readers for their crucial notes on the book: Matthew LeHew, Mike Lars White, Philip J Reed, David L. Craddock, Dennis Burke, Kevin Purdy, Matt Mason, Joseph M. Owens, Stephen Meyerink, Nick Sweeney, and Benjamin Rait.

Thanks to Jason Leung for being so generous with his time and secrets. Thanks to Ken and Nancy Durham, who allowed a conversation about this book to suddenly turn into an on-the-record interview. Thanks to Jane Kernan for helping me understand how the game communicates mystery. Thanks to Joshua Lindquist of Zelda Universe for letting me pick his brain about Zelda and *Majora*'s fan community. Thanks to Victor

Luckerson for turning me onto this game—I don't think I'd have written this book if not for his article, or for the fact that he had to turn down my offer for him to write a *Majora's Mask* book himself.

Thanks to everyone quoted and cited throughout. Thanks to everyone who interviewed *Majora*'s creators through the years, and to everyone who translated those interviews into English.

Thanks to Cory Schmitz for the striking cover, and to Lori Colbeck and Christopher Moyer for the always-pristine layout. Thanks to the following people for their help with Boss Fight Books throughout history: Melissa Malan, Meghan Burklund, Ryan Plummer, Jim Fingal, Maxwell Neely-Cohen, Ken Baumann, Jesse Grce, Adam Robinson, Burkey Kountz, Cameron Daxon, David Wolinsky, Ryan Harvey Pearcy, Cathy Durham, Ed Locke, Brent Lowry, Rebecca Rehfeld, and Delilah the Dog. Thanks to Boss Fight's growing roster of ace authors, and to our kind and curious readers.

SPECIAL THANKS

For making our fifth season of books possible, Boss Fight Books would like to thank John Romero, Ian Chung, Fenric Cayne, Trey Adams, Jennifer Durham-Fowler, Cathy Durham & Ed Locke, Ken Durham & Nancy Magnusson Durham, Nate Mitchell, Lawliet Tamaki Aivazis, Cassandra Newman, seanz0r, Zach Davis, Andrew "Xestrix" Carlson, Ant'ny Fataski, David Goodenough, Adam Hejmowski, Joshua Mallory, and Sean 'Ariamaki' Riedinger.

ALSO FROM
BOSS FIGHT BOOKS